Arabic With Husna

Arabic With Husna is a first of its kind, comprehensive Qur'anic Arabic curriculum that leverages best teaching practices based on experience with thousands of students, enhanced study materials designed to optimize student learning and most importantly video resources in order to ensure a rich, engaging, meticulously organized and result driven learning experience for children and adults alike. This curriculum was put together by a team of educators in collaboration with Ustadh Nouman Ali Khan at the Bayyinah Institute. It is hoped that this approach will revolutionize learning the language of the Qur'an for individuals and educational institutions all over the world, insha Allah.

This Arabic With Husna book is comprised of Modules, Chapters and Lessons. A module is a large, complete concept. A chapter is a subset of a module and covers an important pillar of the module. A lesson is a subset of a chapter and is the smallest piece of a concept that can be covered in one setting (e.g. in one class).

The Arabic instruction needed to complete the lessons is delivered through the Arabic With Husna series on Bayyinah TV. It is also accessible through guided explanations after each chapter. It is recommended to use both Bayyinah TV and the guided explanations for learning purposes.

To sign up for Bayyinah TV, visit www.bayyinah.tv.

Bayyinah Institute
2300 Valley View Lane, Suite 500
Irving, TX 75062

www.bayyinah.tv

ISBN: 978-0-9862750-3-6

Contributors:
Nouman Ali Khan
Aarij Anwer
Anam Bakali
Touqeer Ahmed
Faadhil AbdulHakkim
Ifrah Shareef
Naim Rahman
Hamza Baig
Merusha Nasoordeen
Javeria Khan

MODULE 4
Introduction to Fi'ls

CHAPTER 1

Past Tense
Fi'l always has a tense and inside pronoun. Memorization of past tense Fi'l with the inside pronoun. Recognizing Fi'ls with attached pronouns.

CHAPTER 2

Jumlah Fi'liyyah
Jumlah Fi'liyyah has Fi'l, Faa'il and Maf'ool. Faa'il is always Raf'. Faa'il can be inside pronoun or outside doer. Outside doer has to be Raf' and after the Fi'l. Maf'ool has to be Nasb. Four types of Maf'ool. Attached pronouns.

CHAPTER 3

Present Tense
Memorization of the present tense Fi'l along with the inside pronoun. Translation. Distinguishing between past and present tense. Normal, light, and lightest (only in present tense Fi'ls). Memorization of light and lightest Harf with meaning.

CHAPTER 4

Forbidding
Difference between forbidding and negating. Forbidding is always lightest. How to turn present tense into forbidding. Who can you forbid (2nd person).

CHAPTER 5

Commanding
How to turn present tense into commanding. Who can you command (2nd person). Always lightest. Difference between commanding/forbidding and requesting/suggesting.

CHAPTER 6

Review
Review of Fi'l in past, present, forbidding, and commanding.

CHAPTER 1
Past Tense

Chapter 1

Recall the definition of a Fi'l is a word that is stuck in time: either the past tense or present tense or future tense. Isn't this same as a verb? A verb is essentially one word, e.g. helped. A Fi'l would be "he helped". A Fi'l is comprised of two words:

1) The action/verb – what happened and when (past/present/future), e.g. helped.
2) The doer – who did the action, e.g. he.

The Inside Pronoun

Every Fi'l has a doer. This doer is hidden inside the Fi'l; it isn't even written out explicitly! So the Fi'l نَصَرَ is written as one word, even though there are two words there: he helped.

The doer that is hidden inside the Fi'l is called **the inside pronoun**. This applies to every Fi'l: **there will always be an inside pronoun**.

Examples

نَصَرَ means "He helped"

- The action is "helped". The inside pronoun is "he". The Fi'l is "he helped".
- How can we tell that the inside pronoun is 'he'? The Fatha at the end means that it is هُوَ, he.

نَصَرَتْ means "She helped".

- The action is "helped". The inside pronoun is "she". The Fi'l is "she helped".
- The تْ at the end means the inside pronoun is هِيَ, she.

نَصَرَا (with an Alif, pronounced nasaraaa) means "Both of them helped".

- The action is "helped". The inside pronoun is هُمَا "both of them". The Fi'l is "both of them helped".

From the examples above, notice that:

1) The action used was "helped". This is only because we are using "helped" as our example above. This explains why the letters نصر are present in each example.

2) The different endings of the F'il tell you who the inside pronoun is.

Let us examine some other Fi'l besides "helped" to "help" you understand better.

كَتَبَ – He wrote; كَتَبَتْ – She wrote; كَتَبَا – Both of them wrote.
عَلَّمَ – He taught; عَلَّمَتْ – She taught; عَلَّمَا – Both of them taught.
سَمِعَ – He listened; سَمِعَتْ – She listened; سَمِعَا – Both of them listened.
فَرِحَ – He was happy; فَرِحَتْ – She was happy; فَرِحَا – Both of them were happy.

The Fi'l Madi Chart

In this lesson, we will learn about the past tense Fi'l called Fi'l Madi الفِعْلُ المَاضِي:

	Plural	Pair	Singular	
Masculine	They helped هُمْ نَصَرُوا	Both of them helped هُمَا نَصَرَا	He helped هُوَ نَصَرَ	
	They (f) helped هُنَّ نَصَرْنَ	Both of them (f) helped هُمَا نَصَرَتَا	She helped هِيَ نَصَرَتْ	Feminine
Masculine	You all helped أَنْتُمْ نَصَرْتُمْ	Both of you helped أَنْتُمَا نَصَرْتُمَا	You helped أَنْتَ نَصَرْتَ	
	You all (f) helped أَنْتُنَّ نَصَرْتُنَّ	Both of you (f) helped أَنْتُمَا نَصَرْتُمَا	You (f) helped أَنْتِ نَصَرْتِ	Feminine
For Both Genders	We helped نَحْنُ نَصَرْنَا		I helped أَنَا نَصَرْتُ	

The Fi'l With Attached Pronoun

Remember that there is always an inside pronoun in a Fi'l. At times, you will see a Fi'l with an attached pronoun as well. So how do we translate these Fi'l correctly without mixing up the two pronouns?

1. Identify the attached pronoun and ignore it.
2. Translate the Fi'l with the inside pronoun.
3. Translate the attached pronoun and the Fi'l together.

Application

Let us translate the following Fi'l:

عَلَّمُوْنَا

1. Identify attached pronoun:

   نَا is the attached pronoun version of نَحْنُ. It means 'we'.

2. Translate the Fi'l with the inside pronoun:

   عَلَّمُوْا means 'They taught'

3. Translate the whole thing:

   عَلَّمُوْنَا means 'They taught us'

ضَرَبْتُهُ

1. Identify attached pronoun:

   هُ is the attached pronoun version of هُوَ. It means 'he'.

2. Translate the Fi'l with the inside pronoun:

   ضَرَبْتُ means 'I hit'.

3. ضَرَبْتُهُ means 'I hit him'.

رَأَيْنَك

1. Identify attached pronoun:

   كَ is the attached pronoun version of أَنْتَ. It means 'you'.

2. Translate the Fi'l with the inside pronoun:

   رَأَيْنَ means 'They (f) saw'.

3. Translate the whole thing:

   رَأَيْنَكَ means 'They (f) saw you'.

Date: ______________________________

Lesson 1

Accompanying Video
Unit 1: 1.15.1

Learning Goals
- Know the first half of the past tense conjugation

A

Watch the accompanying video. Based on what you hear and see in the video, write/ circle the correct answer.

1. Fi'l Maadhi means '______________________'.

2. نَصَرَ means '______________________'.

3. The pronoun ______________________ is hiding inside of the Fi'l نَصَرَ.

4. نَصَرَتْ means '______________________'.

5. نَصَرَا means '________________________________'.

6. نَصَرَتَا means '________________________________'.

7. كَتَبَتْ means '________________________________'.

8. آمَنَّا means '________________________________'.

9. نَصَرُوْا means '________________________________'.

10. دَرَسْتَا means '________________________________'.

11. سَمِعُوْا means '________________________________'.

12. نَصَرْنَ means '________________________________'.

13. فَرِحْنَ means '________________________________'.

Date: ____________________

B Fill in the blanks using the word bank.

Wrote	*Doer*	*Status*	*Harf*	*After*	*Helped*	*Studied*
One	*Isms*	كَتَبَ	نَصَرُوْا	دَرَسَتْ	*Fi'l*	*Two*

1. There are three types of words in Arabic: Ism, Fi'l, and ________________.

2. ________________ have four properties: ________________, number, gender, and type.

3. A(n) ________________ is a word stuck in a tense.

4. A Harf is a word that doesn't make any sense unless a word comes ________________ it.

5. Fi'ls are not the same thing as verbs because verbs are just ________________ word, like 'helped.' But Fi'ls are ________________ words because they have the ________________ hidden inside them, like 'He helped.'

6. ________________ is a past tense verb that means 'He ________________'.

7. ________________ is a past tense verb that means 'She ________________'.

8. ________________ is a past tense verb that means 'They ________________'.

Date: ____________________

C

Match the Fi'l to its meaning. They have been divided up so 1-6 match with A-F, 7-12 match with G-L, and 13-15 match with M-O.

A. He helped	1. نَصَرُوْا
B. Both of them studied	2. آمَنَتَا
C. They helped	3. نَصَرَ
D. She believed	4. دَرَسْنَ
E. Both of them (f) believed	5. دَرَسَا
F. They (f) studied	6. آمَنَتْ
G. They believed	7. دَرَسَ
H. They (f) helped	8. آمَنَا
I. He studied	9. آمَنُوْا
J. Both of them (f) helped	10. دَرَسَتْ
K. Both of them believed	11. نَصَرَتَا
L. She studied	12. نَصَرْنَ
M. He helped	13. آمَنَ
N. He studied	14. نَصَرَ
O. He believed	15. دَرَسَ

Date: ______________________

D

Write the independent pronouns in order. Then, write the inside pronoun along with the correct version of دَرَسَ. The first one has been done as an example.

	هُمَا	
		أَنْتَ
أَنْتُنَّ		
		هُوَ دَرَسَ

Date: ____________________

E

Identify the inside pronoun for each Fi'l.

1. فَعَلْتُ ____________
2. جَاءَ ____________
3. نَصَرَ ____________
4. آمَنَا ____________
5. جَعَلَ ____________
6. سَمِعَا ____________
7. رَزَقَا ____________
8. بَشَّرَ ____________
9. جَعَلْتَا ____________
10. عَلَّمْنَ ____________
11. أَنْزَلْتَا ____________
12. آمَنُوْا ____________
13. أَنْزَلَ ____________
14. أَسْلَمَتَا ____________
15. أَنْزَلُوْا ____________
16. بَشَّرَتْ ____________
17. جَائَتْ ____________
18. أَنْذَرُوْا ____________
19. أَنْذَرْنَ ____________
20. أَفْلَحتْ ____________
21. أَنْزَلْتُ ____________
22. جَعَلَا ____________
23. آمَنَتْ ____________
24. بَشَّرُوْا ____________
25. نَصَرَتَا ____________
26. أَسْلَمْنَ ____________
27. أَنْذَرَ ____________
28. كَتَبَتَا ____________
29. عَلَّمَتْ ____________
30. حَسِبَتْ ____________

Date: ______________________

F

Translate the Fi'ls into Arabic using the word bank.

To write	كَتَبَ	To warn	أَنْذَرَ	To assume	حَسِبَ
To study	دَرَسَ	To say	قَالَ	To believe	آمَنَ
To teach	عَلَّمَ	To make	جَعَلَ	To congratulate	بَشَّرَ

1. He wrote

____

2. Both of them warned

____

3. They said

____

4. She taught

____

5. Both of them (f) assumed

____

6. They (f) congratulated

____

7. He made

____

8. She studied

____

9. They believed

____

10. They (f) taught

____

Date: ____________________

Lesson 2

Accompanying Video
Unit 1: 1.15.2

Learning Goals • Memorize all past tense conjugation • Identify the inside pronoun for Fi'ls

A

Watch the accompanying video. Based on what you hear and see in the video, write/circle the correct answer.

1. سَمِعْتَ means '____________________'.

2. آمَنَّ means '____________________'.

3. آمَنْتُنَّ means '____________________'.

4. آمَنْتُ means '____________________'.

5. آمَنَّا means '____________________'.

6. دَرَسْنَ means '____________________'.

7. كَتَبْتُمْ means '____________________'.

8. 'Both of those women studied' would be translated as '____________________'.

9. 'You (feminine) helped' would be translated as '____________________'.

10. 'I believed' would be translated as '____________________'.

Date: ____________________

B

Match the Fi'l to its meaning.

A. He wrote	1. نَصَرَا
B. Both of them helped	2. نَصَرَتَا
C. They believed	3. نَصَرْتِ
D. She studied	4. كَتَبَ
E. Both of them (f) helped	5. كَتَبْتُمَا
F. They (f) made	6. كَتَبْنَا
G. You believed	7. آمَنُوا
H. Both of you wrote	8. آمَنْتَ
I. All of you studied	9. آمَنْتُ
J. You (f) helped	10. دَرَسَتْ
K. All of you (f) made	11. دَرَسْتُمْ
L. I believed	12. جَعَلْنَ
M. We wrote	13. جَعَلْتُنَّ

Date: ____________________

C

Write the conjugation for سَمِعَ.

هُوَ ____________ هُمَا ____________ هُمْ ____________

هِيَ ____________ هُمَا ____________ هُنَّ ____________

أَنْتَ ____________ أَنْتُمَا ____________ أَنْتُمْ ____________

أَنْتِ ____________ أَنْتُمَا ____________ أَنْتُنَّ ____________

أَنَا ____________ نَحْنُ ____________

Date: ____________

D Identify the inside pronoun for each Fi'l.

1. سَمِعْتُمْ ________
2. نَصَرْنَا ________
3. آمَنَّا ________
4. جَعَلْنَ ________
5. سَمِعْتِ ________
6. رَزَقْتُ ________
7. رَزَقَا ________
8. بَشَّرْنَ ________
9. جَعَلُوْا ________
10. أَنْذَرْنَا ________
11. كَتَبْتُمَا ________
12. آمَنُوْا ________
13. أَسْلَمَتَا ________
14. ذَهَبْتَ ________
15. أَنْزَلُوْا ________
16. بَشَّرْتُنَّ ________
17. جَاءَتْ ________
18. أَنْذَرْتُمْ ________
19. أَنْذَرْتُ ________
20. أَفْلَحْتَ ________
21. أَنْزَلَ ________
22. جَعَلْنَا ________
23. آمَنَتْ ________
24. بَشَّرُوْا ________
25. نَصَرْتِ ________
26. أَسْلَمْتُمْ ________
27. أَنْذَرَتَا ________
28. كَتَبْتُنَّ ________
29. عَلَّمَتْ ________
30. حَسِبْتَ ________

Date: ______________________

E Write the conjugation for جَعَلَ.

هُمْ ________	هُمَا ________	هُوَ ________
هُنَّ ________	هُمَا ________	هِيَ ________
أَنْتُمْ ________	أَنْتُمَا ________	أَنْتَ ________
أَنْتُنَّ ________	أَنْتُمَا ________	أَنْتِ ________
	نَحْنُ ________	أَنَا ________

Date: ____________________

F

Translate the Fi'ls into English using the word bank.

To write	كَتَبَ	To warn	أَنْذَرَ	To assume	حَسِبَ
To study	دَرَسَ	To say	قَالَ	To believe	آمَنَ
To teach	عَلَّمَ	To make	جَعَلَ	To congratulate	بَشَّرَ

1. بَشَّرْتُمَا

____

2. آمَنُوا

____

3. قَالَتْ

____

4. أَنْذَرْتُمْ

____

5. حَسِبْنَ

____

6. عَلَّمْتَ

____

7. دَرَسَا

____

8. كَتَبْتُ

____

9. جَعَلْتُنَّ

____

10. دَرَسْنَا

____

Date: ____________________

G | Translate the Fi'ls into Arabic using the word bank.

1. He believed

____

2. She congratulated

____

3. Both of them taught

____

4. They warned

____

5. They (f) wrote

____

6. You assumed

____

7. Both of you made

____

8. All of you believed

____

9. You (f) wrote

____

10. All of you (f) studied

____

11. I assumed

____

12. We believed

____

Date: ____________________

Lesson 3

Accompanying Video
Unit 1: 1.15.3

Learning Goals
- Practice identifying the inside pronoun for of a Fi'l

A

Watch the accompanying video. Based on what you hear and see in the video, write/ circle the correct answer.

1. The inside pronoun for أَنْفَقْتُ is ________________.

2. سَاعَدُوْا means '____________________'.

3. The inside pronoun for بَشَّرْنَ is ________________.

4. The inside pronoun for اِسْتَنَدْتُمْ is ________________.

5. تَعَلَّمْتُنَّ means '________________________________'.

6. The inside pronoun for حَسِبْتَا is ________________.

7. عَمِلْتُ means '____________________'.

8. The inside pronoun for أَنْفَقْتِ is ________________.

9. جَعَلْتَ means '____________________'.

10. The inside pronoun for اِسْتَغْفَرْتُمْ is ________________.

Date: ____________________

B | Identify the inside pronoun for each Fi'l then translate the pronoun.

1. خَلَقَ ______ هُوَ ______ He ______

2. عَمِلُوْا ______ ______

3. جَمَعْتِ ______ ______

4. بَلَغَتَا ______ ______

5. كُنْتُمْ ______ ______

6. زُلْزِلَتْ ______ ______

7. رَزَقَ ______ ______

8. أَنزَلْنَا ______ ______

9. حَسِبْتَ ______ ______

10. أَنْذَرْتُ ______ ______

Date: ____________________

11. عَلِمْتُمْ ____________ ____________________

12. آمَنَّا ____________ ____________________

13. عَلَّمْتَ ____________ ____________________

14. بَلَغْنَ ____________ ____________________

15. سَمِعْتُمَا ____________ ____________________

16. ذَهَبْتِ ____________ ____________________

17. كَتَبَا ____________ ____________________

18. بَشَّرَتْ ____________ ____________________

19. جَعَلُوا ____________ ____________________

20. ظَلَمْتُنَّ ____________ ____________________

Date: ______________________

Lesson 4

Accompanying Video
Unit 1: 1.15.4

Learning Goals • Attach pronouns to Fi'ls • Practice translating Fi'ls with attached pronouns

A

Watch the accompanying video. Based on what you hear and see in the video, write/circle the correct answer.

1. The attached pronoun in فَهِمَتْنِي is ______________.

2. The attached pronoun in عَلَّمُوْنَا is ______________.

3. The attached pronoun in ضَرَبْتُهُ is ______________.

4. رَأَيْنَكَ means '____'.

5. سَاعَدَتَانَا means '____'.

6. اِسْتَغْفَرْتِهِ means '____'.

7. أَكَلُوْهَا means '____'.

8. أَنْزَلْنَاهُ means '____'.

9. أَمَرْتَنِي means '____'.

10. حَاجَّهُ means '____'.

11. نَصَرْتُمُوْهُ means '____'.

12. Anytime a pronoun is attached to a Fi'l, it is in ______________ status because it is a detail.

Date: ______________________

B

Write the attached pronouns in order. If there are two versions, be sure to write both.

______	هُمَا|هِمَا	______
______	______	______
______	______	كَ
كُنَّ	______	______
	______	______

Date: ____________________

C

Attach each pronoun in order to the Fi'l نَصَرَتْ, then translate.
Hint: The Fi'l doesn't change, the attached pronoun changes. So the translation will always start with 'She helped...'.

نَصَرَتْهُ

She helped him

نَصَرَتْكُمَا

She helped both of you

Date: ____________________

D

Identify the inside pronoun for each Fi’l (the doer) and the attached pronoun (the detail).

	Detail	Doer
1. خَلَقَكُمْ	كُمْ	هُوَ
2. فَهِمَتْنِي	________	________
3. جَمَعْنَكُمَا	________	________
4. عَلَّمُونَا	________	________
5. أَرْسَلْتُنَّكِ	________	________
6. ضَرَبْتُهُمَا	________	________
7. وَجَدْتَهُمْ	________	________
8. أَنْزَلَاهَا	________	________
9. كَتَبْتِهِ	________	________
10. أَنْذَرْنَاكَ	________	________

Date: ____________________

E

Identify the inside pronoun for each Fi'l (the doer) and the attached pronoun (the detail) and write the English translation of each pronoun.

	Doer	Detail
1. خَلَقَكُمْ	He	All of you
2. اِسْتَغْفَرْتِهِ		
3. ضَرَبْتُكَ		
4. جَعَلْنَاهَا		
5. اِنْتَظَرَتَاهُمَا		
6. سَاعَدْتُهُنَّ		
7. عَلَّمْتُكُنَّ		
8. أَرْسَلَاكِ		
9. وَجَدْنَنَا		
10. دَرَّسْتُمُوهُمْ		

Date: ______________________

F

Translate the Fi'ls into English using the word bank.

To write	كَتَبَ	To warn	أَنْذَرَ	To assume	حَسِبَ
To study	دَرَسَ	To help	نَصَرَ	To believe	آمَنَ
To teach	عَلَّمَ	To make	جَعَلَ	To congratulate	بَشَّرَ

1. نَصَرَكُمَا

____

2. حَسِبْتَهُ

____

3. نَصَرُوْنِي

____

4. عَلَّمْتُنَّهُمْ

____

5. أَنْذَرَتَاكُمْ

____

6. بَشَّرْتُكُنَّ

____

7. كَتَبْنَهَا

____

8. أَنْذَرْتِهِمَا

____

9. جَعَلْتُمُوْهَا

____

10. دَرَسْتُمَاهُ

____

Date: ____________________

G Translate the Fi'ls into Arabic using the word bank.

1. She wrote it

2. He congratulated both of them

3. Both of them taught us

4. They warned you

5. They (f) congratulated me

6. They taught all of you (f)

7. Both of you warned them

8. All of you taught me

9. You (f) made it (f)

10. All of you warned them

11. We helped both of them

12. I taught her

Date: ____________________

Lesson 5

Accompanying Video
Unit 1: 1.15.5

Learning Goals
- Practice translating past tense Fi'ls with attached pronouns

A

Watch the accompanying video. Based on what you hear and see in the video, write/circle the correct answer.

1. حَسِبْتَاهُ means '________________________________'.

2. عَلِمْتُكُمَا means '________________________________'.

3. In أَخْرَجْتُمُوْنِي, the extra و is added because the Arabs think it sounds smoother than to say أَخْرَجْتُمْنِي, this will always be the case anytime a pronoun is attached to a Fi'l that ends with تُمْ. أَخْرَجْتُمُوْنِي means '________________________'.

4. أَنْفَقْتِهِ means 'you (feminine) spent it'.

5. جَعَلْتَهُنَّ means '________________________________'.

6. بَشَّرْتُمَاهَا means '________________________________'.

7. اِسْتَغْفَرْتُمُوْهُ means '________________________________'.

Date: ____________________

B

Conjugate the Fi'l نَصَرَ with the attached pronoun هَا, then translate.
Hint: The Fi'l changes, but the attached pronoun doesn't. So the translation will always end with '...helped her'.

نَصَرَهَا

He helped her

نَصَرْتُمَاهَا

Both of you helped her

Date: ______________________

C

Attach each pronoun in order to the Fi'l نَظَرْتُ, then translate.
Hint: The Fi'l doesn't change, the attached pronoun changes. So the translation will always start with 'I saw...'.

نَظَرْتُهُ

I saw him

نَظَرْتُكُمَا

I saw both of you

Date: ____________________

D

Identify the inside pronoun and the attached pronoun, then translate it to complete the translation given.

1. ___He___ created ___all of you___ خَلَقَكُمْ .1

2. ________ hit ________ ضَرَبْتُمَانِي .2

3. ________ helped ________ سَاعَدُوْنَا .3

4. ________ praised ________ حَمِدَاكَ .4

5. ________ ate ________ أَكَلْنَاهُ .5

6. ________ fed ________ أَطْعَمَتَاكُنَّ .6

7. ________ thanked ________ شَكَرْتِهِنَّ .7

8. ________ heard ________ سَمِعْتُنَّهُ .8

9. ________ honored ________ كَرَّمْتُهَا .9

10. ________ taught ________ عَلَّمَتْكِ .10

Date: ______________________

11. ______________ saw ______________ رَأَيْتُكُمَا .11

12. ______________ congratulated ______________ بَشَّرْنَكَ .12

13. ______________ placed ______________ وَضَعَهُ .13

14. ______________ sent ______________ أَرْسَلُوْهُمَا .14

15. ______________ preferred ______________ فَضَّلْتُكُمْ .15

16. ______________ waited for ______________ اِنْتَظَرْتِهِمَا .16

17. ______________ respected ______________ وَقَّرْتُمُوْنِي .17

18. ______________ guided ______________ هَدَيْنَاهُمْ .18

19. ______________ saw ______________ نَظَرْتَنَا .19

20. ______________ paid ______________ أَنْقَدْنَكُنَّ .20

Date: ____________________

Qur'anic Application

Identify if each highlighted word below is a past tense Fi'l. If it is, identify its inside pronoun.

تَبَارَكَ الَّذِي بِيَدِهِ الْمُلْكُ وَهُوَ عَلَىٰ كُلِّ شَيْءٍ **قَدِيرٌ** ﴿١﴾ الَّذِي **خَلَقَ** الْمَوْتَ وَالْحَيَاةَ

لِيَبْلُوَكُمْ أَيُّكُمْ **أَحْسَنُ** عَمَلًا ۚ وَهُوَ **الْعَزِيزُ** الْغَفُورُ ﴿٢﴾ الَّذِي **خَلَقَ** سَبْعَ

سَمَاوَاتٍ طِبَاقًا ۖ مَّا تَرَىٰ فِي **خَلْقِ** الرَّحْمَٰنِ مِن تَفَاوُتٍ ۖ فَارْجِعِ **الْبَصَرَ** هَلْ تَرَىٰ مِن

فُطُورٍ ﴿٣﴾ ثُمَّ ارْجِعِ الْبَصَرَ **كَرَّتَيْنِ** يَنقَلِبْ إِلَيْكَ الْبَصَرُ خَاسِئًا وَهُوَ **حَسِيرٌ** ﴿٤﴾

وَلَقَدْ **زَيَّنَّا** السَّمَاءَ الدُّنْيَا بِمَصَابِيحَ وَ**جَعَلْنَاهَا** رُجُومًا لِّلشَّيَاطِينِ ۖ وَ**أَعْتَدْنَا** لَهُمْ

عَذَابَ **السَّعِيرِ** ﴿٥﴾ وَلِلَّذِينَ **كَفَرُوا** بِرَبِّهِمْ عَذَابُ جَهَنَّمَ ۖ وَبِئْسَ الْمَصِيرُ ﴿٦﴾

CHAPTER 2
Jumlah Fi'liyyah

Chapter 2

Recall that the doer that is hidden inside the Fi'l is called the inside pronoun. Thus, when we translate a Fi'l, we translate it as "he helped", "I learned", "she saw", etc. However, what if we wanted to say, "Muhammad helped", "My friend learned", "Aisha saw"? In this case, we would require an outside doer.

Examples

نَصَرَ مُحَمَّدٌ

Muhammad helped

نَصَرَ صَدِيقِي

My friend helped

نَصَرَتْ عَائِشَةُ

Aisha helped

The Outside Doer

"Muhammad", "My friend", "Aisha" in the above examples are called outside doers. Why call them outside doers? Unlike the inside pronoun, they are written explicitly outside of the Fi'l.

Did you notice that we dropped the inside pronoun from the translations above? When we had نَصَرَ, we translate it as "he helped". However, نَصَرَ مُحَمَّدٌ is translated as "Muhammad helped", excluding "he".

When you have an outside doer, it replaces the inside pronoun in meaning.

Rules for the Outside Doer

1) The outside doer must come after the Fi'l (not necessarily right after).
2) It must be in Raf' status.
3) The inside pronoun must be he هُوَ or she هِيَ.

Application

Let us translate the following sentences:

نَصَرَ اللهُ

✓ Outside Doer

✓ The outside doer must come after the Fi'l

✓ Raf' status

✓ Inside pronoun is he هُوَ

Translation: Allah helped.

نَصَرَ اللهَ

× Outside Doer

✓ The outside doer must come after the Fi'l

× Raf' status

Translation: He helped Allah.

Note: Since there is no outside doer, we go back to the inside pronoun for the translation.

اللهُ نَصَرَ

× Outside Doer

× The outside doer must come after the Fi'l

✓ Raf' status

✓ Inside pronoun is he هُوَ

Translation: **Allah**, he helped.

The Jumlah Fi'liyyah

Recall that there are two types of sentences in Arabic:

1) Jumlah Ismiyyah الجُمْلَةُ الاِسْمِيَّةُ – a sentence that begins with an Ism in Raf' status; it has the invisible "is".
2) Jumlah Fi'liyyah الجُمْلَةُ الفِعْلِيَّةُ – anytime you have a Fi'l, you have a Jumlah Fi'liyyah.

Parts of a Jumlah Fi'liyyah

Jumlah Fi'liyyah is a sentence that has three parts:

1) Fi'l فِعْل – the action.
2) Faa'il فَاعِل – the doer of the action, could be an inside pronoun or outside doer.
3) The Maf'ool مَفْعُوْل – the details of the action.

Examples

وَقَتَلَ دَاوُودُ جَالُوتَ

And David killed Goliath.

1) Fi'l – قَتَلَ killed
2) Faa'il – دَاوُودُ David (outside doer)
3) The Maf'ool – جَالُوتَ Goliath

وَأَنْزَلَ الْفُرْقَانَ

And He sent down the criterion.

1) Fi'l – أَنْزَلَ sent down
2) Faa'il – هُوَ he (inside pronoun)
3) The Maf'ool – الْفُرْقَانَ the criterion

Rules for Jumlah Fi'liyyah

1) The Faa'il فَاعِل always has to be in Raf' status.
2) The Maf'ool مَفْعُول always has to be in Nasb status.
3) The Faa'il فَاعِل can be an inside pronoun or outside doer.

4) The Maf'ool مَفْعُول can be an attached pronoun or an Ism explicitly written out.

5) You always need a Fi'l فِعْل and a Faa'il فَاعِل. The Maf'ool مَفْعُول is not always required.

Different Types of Maf'ool

There can be more than one Maf'ool مَفْعُول in the sentence. Furthermore, different types of مَفْعُوْل answer different kinds of questions. Below is a list of the different types of مَفْعُوْل and what questions they answer:

- مَفْعُوْلٌ بِهِ: Who/What the action was done to
- مَفْعُوْلٌ فِيْه: When/Where the action took place
- مَفْعُوْلٌ حَالٌ: How did the action take place
- مَفْعُوْلٌ لَهُ: Why did the action take place

Date: ____________________

Lesson 1

Accompanying Video
Unit 1: 1.16.1

Learning Goals • Know when an outside doer is possible • Identify outside doers

A

Watch the accompanying video. Based on what you hear and see in the video, write/circle the correct answer.

1. In the Fi'l نَصَرَ the pronoun هُوَ is the inside pronoun of the Fi'l, so هُوَ is the ______________.

2. The only times you may get a(n) ______________ doer is when you see the هُوَ version of a Fi'l (like نَصَرَ) or the هِيَ version (like نَصَرَتْ).

3. When you have a Fi'l (هُوَ or هِيَ versions only) followed by an Ism that is in Raf' status, then that Ism fires the inside pronoun and becomes the outside doer. نَصَرَ الْمُسْلِمُ would be translated as '______________________________'.

4. The two rules for the outside doer are that it must be ______________ the Fi'l and it must be in Raf' status.

5. نَصَرَكُمُ اللهُ means '______________________________'.

6. دَرَسَ الْمُسْلِمَانِ is a correct statement because even though دَرَسَ is singular and اَلْمُسْلِمَانِ is pair, اَلْمُسْلِمَانِ still meets the requirements to be an outside ______________.

7. أَكَلَتْ بَنَاتٌ means '______________________________'.

Date: ______________________

B | Fill in the blanks using the word bank.

Plural	*Outside*	*Two*	*Inside*	*Raf'*	*After*
نَصَرَ	هُوَ	نَصَرَتْ	نَصَرُوْا	اَلْعَامِلَةُ	هِيَ

1. There are two types of doers: an inside pronoun and a(n) ______________ doer.

2. The inside pronoun of a Fi'l is called the ______________ doer.

3. There are only ______________ times a word can have an outside doer.

4. You can only look for an outside doer when a Fi'l has the inside pronoun ______________ or ______________.

5. ______________ can have an outside doer. ______________ can't have an outside doer.

6. The outside doer must be ______________ and must come ______________ the Fi'l.

7. In the phrase نَصَرَتْ اَلْعَامِلَةُ الزَّائِرَةَ, ______________ is the outside doer.

8. The Fi'l and outside doer don't have to match in number. Even if the outside doer is dual or ______________, the Fi'l still stays in the هُوَ or هِيَ versions.

9. The gender of the Fi'l has to match the gender of the outside doer. To say, 'The two female workers helped the Muslims', you would say اَلْعَامِلَتَانِ الْمُسْلِمِينَ ______________.

Date: ____________________

C

Circle the Fi'l that can have an outside doer.

1. A. نَصَرَ
   B. نَصَرَتَا
   C. نَصَرْتُ
   D. نَصَرُوْا

2. A. كَتَبْتُمْ
   B. كَتَبْتُ
   C. كَتَبَتْ
   D. كَتَبْنَا

3. A. سَاعَدَا
   B. سَاعَدْنَ
   C. سَاعَدْتِ
   D. سَاعَدَتْ

4. A. ذَهَبُوْا
   B. ذَهَبْتُنَّ
   C. ذَهَبَ
   D. ذَهَبْنَا

5. A. هَدَيْتَ
   B. هَدَيْتُ
   C. هَدَتْ
   D. هَدَيْنَ

6. A. اِسْتَفْسَرَتْ
   B. اِسْتَفْسَرْتُنَّ
   C. اِسْتَفْسَرَا
   D. اِسْتَفْسَرَتَا

7. A. تَغَيَّرَ
   B. تَغَيَّرَا
   C. تَغَيَّرْتَ
   D. تَغَيَّرْتُمْ

8. A. قُلْتَ
   B. قَالَتَا
   C. قُلْتُ
   D. قَالَ

9. A. وَضَعْتُمَا
   B. كَرُمْتَا
   C. غَادَرَتْ
   D. صَلَّيْنَا

10. A. أَسْلَمْتُ
    B. سَمِعَتَا
    C. اِتَّخَذْنَ
    D. اِقْتَرَبَ

11. A. وَجَدْتِ
    B. حَفِظْتَ
    C. أَكَلَتْ
    D. اِسْتَيْقَظْنَ

12. A. شَرِبْتِ
    B. حَاوَلْنَ
    C. اِسْتَعَانَ
    D. خِفْتَ

Date: ______________________

D

Identify if the word after the Fi'l is the outside doer. If not, write why not.
Hint: Remember, to have an outside doer the inside pronoun must be هُوَ or هِيَ. The word must also be after the Fi'l, in Raf' status, and the same gender as the Fi'l.

1. نَصَرَ الْمُسْلِمُ ______________________
2. جَاءَ الزَّابِرُونَ ______________________
3. دَخَلَ الْبَيْتَ ______________________
4. أَنْزَلَا الْأُسْتَاذُ ______________________
5. اَلطَّالِبُ دَرَسَ ______________________
6. سَمِعَتْ الْمُعَلِّمَةُ ______________________
7. آمَنَ الْمُؤْمِنُ ______________________
8. خَرَجَتْ الْحَافِظَاتُ ______________________
9. تَكَلَّمَ مُهَنْدِسَةٌ ______________________
10. أَنْذَرَ الْعَامِلِينَ ______________________

Date: ______________________

E

Circle the correct answer in each of the following that has an outside doer. Remember the two Fi'ls that can have outside doers and what status and gender the outside doer must be in.

1. A. نَصَرَ الْمُسْلِمَةُ
   B. نَصَرَتَا الْمُسْلِمَتَانِ
   C. نَصَرَتْ الْمُسْلِمَةُ
   D. نَصَرُوْا الْمُسْلِمُوْنَ

2. A. عَلَّمْنَ الْمُعَلِّمَاتُ
   B. عَلَّمْتَ الْمُعَلِّمَةُ
   C. عَلَّمَ الْمُعَلِّمُ
   D. عَلَّمَ الْمُعَلِّمَةُ

3. A. أَسْلَمَتْ الْعَامِلُوْنَ
   B. أَسْلَمْتَ الْعَامِلُوْنَ
   C. أَسْلَمَتْ الْعَامِلُ
   D. أَسْلَمَتْ الْعَامِلَاتُ

4. A. دَرَّسَتْ الْأُسْتَاذُ
   B. دَرَّسْتَ الْأُسْتَاذَةُ
   C. دَرَّسَتْ الْأُسْتَاذَةُ
   D. دَرَّسَ الْأُسْتَاذَةُ

5. A. أَكَلَا رَجُلَانِ
   B. أَكَلَ رَجُلَانِ
   C. أَكَلَا رَجُلٌ
   D. أَكَلَ رَجُلٍ

6. A. شَكَرَ شَيْخاً
   B. شَكَرَ شَيْخٌ
   C. شَكَرُوْا شَيْخَيْنِ
   D. شَكَرَ شَيْخَيْنِ

7. A. تَعَاوَنَا الطَّبِيبَتَانِ
   B. تَعَاوَنَ الطَّبِيبَتَانِ
   C. تَعَاوَنَ الطَّبِيبَتَيْنِ
   D. تَعَاوَنَتْ الطَّبِيبَتَانِ

8. A. غَادَرَ الْمُوَظَّفِيْنَ
   B. غَادَرَ الْمُوَظَّفُوْنَ
   C. غَادَرُوْا الْمُوَظَّفُوْنَ
   D. غَادَرُوْا الْمُوَظَّفِيْنَ

9. A. بَنَى الْمَسَاجِدُ
   B. بَنَتْ الْمَسْجِدُ
   C. بُنِيَ الْمَسَاجِدُ
   D. بُنِيَتْ الْمَسَاجِدُ

10. A. أَمْطَرَ السَّمَاءُ
    B. أَمْطَرَتْ اَلسَّمَاءُ
    C. أَمْطَرَ السَّمَاوَاتُ
    D. أَمْطَرَتْ اَلسَّمَاوَاتِ

11. A. سَافَرُوْا الْمُسَافِرُوْنَ
    B. أَحْسَنَ الْمُحْسِنُوْنَ
    C. عَبَدَ الْعَابِدِيْنَ
    D. اَنْذَرَا الْمُنْذِرُوْنَ

12. A. قَالَتْ الْمُبَشِّرُ
    B. دَرَسَتْ الطَّالِبَةَ
    C. قَرَأَ الْحَافِظَانِ
    D. أَفْلَحَ السَّابِقَاتُ

Date: ____________________

F

Translate the Fi'ls into English using the word bank.

To write	كَتَبَ	To warn	أَنْذَرَ	To assume	حَسِبَ
To study	دَرَسَ	To help	نَصَرَ	To hit	ضَرَبَ
To teach	عَلَّمَ	To make	جَعَلَ	To congratulate	بَشَّرَ

1. حَسِبَ

____

2. حَسِبَ الْمُسْلِمُ

____

3. حَسِبَ الْمُسْلِمَانِ

____

4. حَسِبَ الْمُسْلِمُوْنَ

____

5. عَلَّمَتْهُمَا

____

6. عَلَّمَتْهُمَا الْمُعَلِّمَةُ

____

7. عَلَّمَتْهُمَا الْمُعَلِّمَتَانِ

____

8. عَلَّمَتْهُمَا الْمُعَلِّمَاتُ

____

9. عَلَّمَتْ الْمُعَلِّمَةُ الطَّالِبَةَ

____

10. عَلَّمَ الْمُعَلِّمُوْنَ الطَّالِبِيْنَ

____

Date: ______________________

G | Translate the Fi'ls into Arabic using the word bank.

1. He made it

____

2. A Muslim made it

____

3. The two Muslims made it

____

4. The Muslims made it

____

5. She congratulated her

____

6. The Muslim woman congratulated her

____

7. Two Muslim women congratulated her

____

8. The Muslim women congratulated her

____

9. You studied

____

10. He studied it

____

11. All of you studied it

____

12. A student studied it

____

Date: ____________________

Lesson 2

Accompanying Video
Unit 1: 1.16.2

Learning Goals
- Practice translating Fi'ls with outside doers

A

Watch the accompanying video. Based on what you hear and see in the video, write/ circle the correct answer.

1. The doer in جَعَلْنَا الْبَيْتَ is ________________.

2. The doer in آمَنَ النَّاسُ is ________________.

3. The doer in الْمُؤْمِنُونَ خَرَجُوْا is ________________.

4. أَنْذَرْتُكُمْ means '________________________________'.

5. حَسِبَتْهُ means '________________________________'.

6. جَعَلَ اللهُ means '______________________'.

7. The doer in تَسَاءَلَ الْمُشْرِكُوْنَ is ______________________.

8. ضَرَبَ الرَّجُلَ مُوسَى means '________________________________'.

9. The doer in اِقْتَرَبَتِ السَّاعَةُ is ________________.

10. شَغَلَتْ is feminine because its doer, أَمْوَالُ, is a(n) ________________________________, thus making it singular and feminine.

11. خَشِيَ الْأَسَدَ الرَّجُلُ means '____'.

12. بَشَّرَ الْمُسْلِمِيْنَ means '____'.

Date: ____________________

B Translate into English with the help of the definitions given.

	Translation	
Sent down: أَنْزَلَ	____________________	1. أَنْزَلَ الْكِتَابَ
Made: جَعَلَ	____________________	2. جَعَلْنَا الْبَيْتَ
Believed: آمَنَ	____________________	3. آمَنَ النَّاسُ
Warned: أَنْذَرَ	____________________	4. أَنْذَرْتُكُمْ
Hit: ضَرَبَ	____________________	5. ضَرَبَ الرَّجُلُ مُوسَى
Wrote: كَتَبَ	____________________	6. كَتَبَ رَبُّكُمْ
Helped: نَصَرَ	____________________	7. نَصَرَ الْمُعَلِّمُ الطَّالِبَ
Congratulated: بَشَّرَ	____________________	8. بَشَّرَتْ الْمُسْلِمِينَ
Saw: رَأَى	____________________	9. رَأَى الرَّجُلُ بَيْتِي
Studied: دَرَسَ	____________________	10. دَرَسَتْ الطَّالِبَةُ

Date: ____________________

Translation

11. قَتَلْتُمْ نَفْسًا ____________________ Killed: قَتَلَ

12. قَالَ رَبُّكَ ____________________ Said: قَالَ

13. عَلَّمَ آدَمَ ____________________ Taught: عَلَّمَ

14. رَزَقَهُمُ اللَّهُ ____________________ Provided for: رَزَقَ

15. عَلَّمْتَنَا ____________________ Taught: عَلَّمَ

16. اِتَّخَذَ اللَّهُ إِبْرَاهِيمَ ____________________ Take: اِتَّخَذَ

17. رَزَقْنَاهُمْ ____________________ Provided for: رَزَقَ

18. بَشَّرْنَاهَا ____________________ Congratulated: بَشَّرَ

19. دَرَسْتَهُ ____________________ Studied: دَرَسَ

20. جَعَلَ مُسْلِمُ الْمَسْجِدَ ____________________ Made: جَعَلَ

Date: ______________________

Lesson 3

Accompanying Video
Unit 1: 1.16.3

Learning Goals • Know the parts of a Jumlah Fi'liyyah • Know the different kinds of Maf'ools

A

Watch the accompanying video. Based on what you hear and see in the video, write/circle the correct answer.

1. A Jumlah Fi'liyyah, a sentence made up of a Fi'l, can have three parts, the فِعْلٌ, فَاعِلٌ, and the مَفْعُوْلٌ. The فِعْلٌ is the act itself, the فَاعِلٌ is the ______________, and the مَفْعُوْلٌ is the detail.

2. Details answer different kinds of ______________.

3. مَفْعُوْلٌ بِهِ answers the question of 'who?' or '______________?'.

4. مَفْعُوْلٌ فِيْهِ answers the question of 'when?' or '______________?'.

5. مَفْعُوْلٌ لَهُ answers the question of '______________?'.

6. مَفْعُوْلٌ حَال answers the question of '______________?'.

7. In the sentence 'I ate your cupcake quickly, yesterday, outside, because I like to', the فَاعِلٌ is '______________'.

8. In the above sentence, the مَفْعُوْلٌ بِهِ is '______________'.

9. In the above sentence, the مَفْعُوْلٌ حَال is '______________'.

10. In the above sentence, the مَفْعُوْلٌ فِيْهِ are 'yesterday' and '______________'.

Date: ___________________

B

Fill in the blanks using the word bank.

Why	*What*	*Quickly*	*Doer*	*Yesterday*	*Her*	*Where*
Met	*Act*	فِعْلٌ	فَاعِلٌ	*Detail*	*I*	*How*

1. A Jumlah Fi'liyyah is a sentence that starts with a(n) _______________.

2. A Jumlah Fi'liyyah has three parts: the فِعْلٌ, the _______________, and the مَفْعُوْلٌ.

3. The فِعْلٌ is the _______________, the فَاعِلٌ is the _______________, and the مَفْعُوْلٌ is the _______________.

4. There are different kinds of Maf'ools. A مَفْعُوْلٌ بِهِ answers 'who?' or '_______________?'. A مَفْعُوْلٌ فِيهِ answers 'when?' or '_______________?'. A مَفْعُوْلٌ لَهُ answers '_______________?'. A مَفْعُوْلٌ حَالٌ answers '_______________?'.

5. In the sentence, 'I met her quickly yesterday', '_______________' is the فَاعِلٌ, '_______________' is the فِعْلٌ, '_______________' is the مَفْعُوْلٌ بِهِ, '_______________' is the مَفْعُوْلٌ حَالٌ, and '_______________' is the مَفْعُوْلٌ فِيهِ.

Date: ______________________

C

Square the Fi'l, circle the Faa'il, and underline the Maf'ools. Be sure to underline each Maf'ool separately.
Hint: Some Maf'ools may be made up of more than one word.

1. The parents gave their children gifts on Eid.
2. We love our mom.
3. The pen fell on the floor.
4. We picked apples from the tree.
5. I visited her after two years.
6. He studied in the library last night for his final exam.
7. The brothers ate eggs in the morning before school because their mom made them.
8. My sister came home early from work yesterday.
9. She runs fast.
10. They completed their homework quickly before dinner.
11. The essay won a prize in the contest.
12. Many people believe her story.
13. She worked hard in school so she could get good grades.
14. You ride your bike with your friend often at the park.
15. The students gave their teacher a gift on the last day of school.
16. They both need a ride.
17. My dad works hard and quickly.
18. Abdullah eats a healthy breakfast everyday at 7 AM so that he can have a productive day.
19. Those guys meet every week at the gym.
20. The doctor treated ten patients today.

Date: ______________________

D

Underline the Maf'ools and label what kind of a Maf'ool it is. Label 'MB' for Maf'ool Bihi, 'MF' for Maf'ool Feehi, 'ML' for Maf'ool Lahu, and 'MH' for Maf'ool Haal. Be sure to underline each Maf'ool seperately.

1. The parents gave <u>their children</u> <u>gifts</u> <u>on Eid</u>.

   MB MB MF

2. I gave her the books this morning so she could read them.

3. She put the bowl of soup on the table very slowly so that it wouldn't spill.

4. We picked delicious red apples carefully from the tree this morning.

5. I visited my friend Maryam and her sister at their home after two years.

6. The students studied their notes in the library all night long for the final exam.

7. The brothers ate eggs in the morning before school because their mom made them.

8. My sister came home early from work yesterday because she was sick.

Date: ____________________

Lesson 4

Accompanying Video
Unit 1: 1.16.4

Learning Goals
- Practice identifying and translating the different parts of a Jumlah Fi'liyyah

A

Watch the accompanying video. Based on what you hear and see in the video, write/ circle the correct answer.

1. In فَوَجَدَا عَبْدًا the word عَبْدًا is a ____________________.
   A. فِعْلٌ *B.* فَاعِلٌ *C.* مَفْعُولٌ بِهِ *D.* مَفْعُولٌ فِيهِ *E.* مَفْعُولٌ لَهُ *F.* مَفْعُولٌ حَال

2. Usually when a pronoun is attached to a Fi'l, it answers the question of 'what?' or 'who?', so it is a ____________________.

3. In رَفَعْنَا فَوْقَكُمُ الطُّورَ the words فَوْقَكُمْ are a ____________________.
   A. فِعْلٌ *B.* فَاعِلٌ *C.* مَفْعُولٌ بِهِ *D.* مَفْعُولٌ فِيهِ *E.* مَفْعُولٌ لَهُ *F.* مَفْعُولٌ حَال

4. In وَجَعَلْنَا بَيْنَهُمَا زَرْعًا the word زَرْعًا is a ____________________.
   A. فِعْلٌ *B.* فَاعِلٌ *C.* مَفْعُولٌ بِهِ *D.* مَفْعُولٌ فِيهِ *E.* مَفْعُولٌ لَهُ *F.* مَفْعُولٌ حَال

5. In آتَيْنَاهُ الْحُكْمَ the word آتَيْنَا is the ____________________.
   A. فِعْلٌ *B.* فَاعِلٌ *C.* مَفْعُولٌ بِهِ *D.* مَفْعُولٌ فِيهِ *E.* مَفْعُولٌ لَهُ *F.* مَفْعُولٌ حَال

6. In خَلَقْنَاكُمْ the word نَحْنُ (from نَا) is the ____________________.
   A. فِعْلٌ *B.* فَاعِلٌ *C.* مَفْعُولٌ بِهِ *D.* مَفْعُولٌ فِيهِ *E.* مَفْعُولٌ لَهُ *F.* مَفْعُولٌ حَال

7. In أَعْتَدْنَا جَهَنَّمَ the word جَهَنَّمَ is a ____________________.

8. In خَرُّوا سُجَّدًا the word سُجَّدًا is a ____________________.
   A. فِعْلٌ *B.* فَاعِلٌ *C.* مَفْعُولٌ بِهِ *D.* مَفْعُولٌ فِيهِ *E.* مَفْعُولٌ لَهُ *F.* مَفْعُولٌ حَال

Date: ______________________

B Translate into English with the help of the definitions.

1. أَنْزَلَ الْكِتَابَ — ___He___ sent down ___the book___

2. وَجَدَا عَبْداً — ______________ found a slave

3. جَعَلْنَا بَيْنَهُمَا زَرْعاً — ______________ made a farm between ______________

4. أَنْذَرْتُكُمْ — ______________ warned ______________

5. آتَيْنَاهُ الْحُكْمَ — ______________ gave ______________ wisdom

6. جَعَلَ مِنْهَا — ______________ made from ______________

7. خَلَقْنَاكُمْ — ______________ created ______________

8. زَيَّنَّا السَّمَاءَ — ______________ beautified the sky

9. عَمِلُوا الصَّالِحَاتِ — ______________ did good deeds

10. خَلَقْنَا الْإِنْسَانَ — ______________ created man

Date: ____________________

11. أَنْعَمْتَ عَلَيْهِمْ ______________ favored upon ______________

12. مَرُّوْا بِهِمْ ______________ passed by ______________

13. نَسِيَا حُوتَهُمَا ______________ forgot ______________ fish

14. لَبِثُوْا فِي كَهْفِهِمْ ______________ remained in ______________ cave

15. ءَاتَتْ أُكُلَهَا ______________ gave ______________ fruit

16. أَخَذَهُ اللّٰهُ ______________ took ______________

17. دَخَلْتَ جَنَّتَكَ ______________ entered ______________ garden

18. اِعْتَزَلْتُمُوْهُمْ ______________ withdrew from ______________

19. فُتِحَتِ السَّمَاءُ ______________ was opened

20. جِئْتُمُوْنَا ______________ came to ______________

Date: ______________________

C | Translate the sentences into English using the word bank.

To take	أَخَذَ	To warn	أَنْذَرَ	To assume	حَسِبَ
To hit	ضَرَبَ	To help	نَصَرَ	To create	خَلَقَ
To teach	عَلَّمَ	To make	جَعَلَ	To look	نَظَرَ

1. أَخَذَهُ

____

2. أَخَذَهَا الْمُسْلِمُ

____

3. أَخَذَهُمُ الْمُسْلِمَانِ

____

4. أَخَذَنِي الْمُسْلِمُوْنَ إِلَى المَسْجِدِ

____

5. ضَرَبْتُهُمَا

____

6. ضَرَبَ الرَّجُلُ

____

7. ضَرَبَ الرَّجُلَ

____

8. جَعَلَتْهُ

____

9. جَعَلْنَا الْبَيْتَ

____

10. جَعَلَ الْمُسْلِمُوْنَ الْبَيْتَ

____

Date: ____________________

D Translate the sentences into Arabic using the word bank.

1. She taught

2. She taught both of them

3. Both of them taught me

4. The Muslim women taught them (f)

5. They (f) taught the Muslim women

6. The two Muslim women taught a man

7. We helped

8. They helped us

9. Both of them helped the teacher

10. The teacher helped both of them

11. The two teachers helped them

12. They helped the two teachers

Date: ____________________

Qur'anic Application

Label each highlighted word below as Fi'l, Faa'il, or Maf'ool.

تَبَارَكَ الَّذِي بِيَدِهِ الْمُلْكُ وَهُوَ عَلَىٰ كُلِّ شَيْءٍ قَدِيرٌ ﴿١﴾ الَّذِي خَلَقَ الْمَوْتَ وَالْحَيَاةَ

لِيَبْلُوَكُمْ أَيُّكُمْ أَحْسَنُ عَمَلًا ۚ وَهُوَ الْعَزِيزُ الْغَفُورُ ﴿٢﴾ الَّذِي خَلَقَ سَبْعَ

سَمَاوَاتٍ طِبَاقًا ۖ مَّا تَرَىٰ فِي خَلْقِ الرَّحْمَٰنِ مِن تَفَاوُتٍ ۖ فَارْجِعِ الْبَصَرَ هَلْ تَرَىٰ مِن

فُطُورٍ ﴿٣﴾ ثُمَّ ارْجِعِ الْبَصَرَ كَرَّتَيْنِ يَنقَلِبْ إِلَيْكَ الْبَصَرُ خَاسِئًا وَهُوَ حَسِيرٌ ﴿٤﴾

وَلَقَدْ زَيَّنَّا السَّمَاءَ الدُّنْيَا بِمَصَابِيحَ وَجَعَلْنَاهَا رُجُومًا لِّلشَّيَاطِينِ ۖ وَأَعْتَدْنَا لَهُمْ

عَذَابَ السَّعِيرِ ﴿٥﴾ وَلِلَّذِينَ كَفَرُوا بِرَبِّهِمْ عَذَابُ جَهَنَّمَ ۖ وَبِئْسَ الْمَصِيرُ ﴿٦﴾

CHAPTER 3
Present Tense

Chapter 3

In chapter 1 we learned about the past tense, Fi'l Madi الفِعْلُ المَاضِي. In this chapter we will learn about the present tense, Fi'l Mudari الفِعْلُ المُضَارِعُ. In terms of sentence structure, all the rules of Jumlah Fi'liyyah جُمْلَةٌ فِعْلِيَّةٌ apply to the present tense.

Unlike the past tense where the changes occur only at the end, in the present tense the changes occur at the beginning or the beginning and the end depending on who the inside pronoun is.

The Fi'l Mudari Chart

	Plural	Pair	Singular	
Masculine	They help هُمْ يَنْصُرُونَ	Both of them help هُمَا يَنْصُرَانِ	He helps هُوَ يَنْصُرُ	
	They (f) help هُنَّ يَنْصُرْنَ	Both of them (f) help هُمَا تَنْصُرَانِ	She hels هِيَ تَنْصُرُ	Feminine
Masculine	You all help أَنْتُمْ تَنْصُرُونَ	Both of you help أَنْتُمَا تَنْصُرَانِ	You help أَنْتَ تَنْصُرُ	
	You all (f) help أَنْتُنَّ تَنْصُرْنَ	Both of you (f) help أَنْتُمَا تَنْصُرَانِ	You (f) help أَنْتِ تَنْصُرِينَ	Feminine
For Both Genders	We help نَحْنُ نَنْصُرُ		I help أَنَا أَنْصُرُ	

Forms of Fi'l Mudari

Recall that a Harf is a word that makes no sense unless a word comes after it. We have seen how Harf Jarr affects its Ism (i.e. makes it Jarr). We have seen how Harf Nasb affects its Ism (i.e. makes it Nasb).

Can a Harf affect a Fi'l? For Fi'l Madi, no. For Fi'l Mudari, yes! Here's how:

1) “Normal”: No Harf is affecting the Fi’l Mudari, so nothing happens.
2) “Light”: The Fi’l loses a Dhamma and gains a Fatha at the end, for a group of Harf (see “The Fi’l Mudari Chart - Light”).
3) “Lightest”: The Fi’l loses a Dhamma and gains a Sukoon at the end, for another group of Harf (see “The Fi’l Mudari Chart - Lightest”).

The Fi’l Mudari Chart – Normal

It is the same as the chart on pg. 73.

The Fi’l Mudari Chart – Light

ن from the normal form is dropped (compare with p. 73)

Fatha

Light Harf Affectng Fil Mudari

Remain Unchanged

هُمْ That they help أَنْ يَنْصُرُوا	هُمَا That both of them help أَنْ يَنْصُرَا	هُوَ That he helps أَنْ يَنْصُرَ
هُنَّ That they (f) help أَنْ يَنْصُرْنَ	هُمَا That both of them (f) help أَنْ تَنْصُرَا	هِيَ That she helps أَنْ تَنْصُرَ
أَنْتُمْ That you all help أَنْ تَنْصُرُوا	أَنْتُمَا That both of you help أَنْ تَنْصُرَا	أَنْتَ That you help أَنْ تَنْصُرَ
أَنْتُنَّ That you all (f) help أَنْ تَنْصُرْنَ	أَنْتُمَا That both of you (f) help أَنْ تَنْصُرَا	أَنْتِ That you (f) help أَنْ تَنْصُرِي
نَحْنُ That we help أَنْ نَنْصُرَ		أَنَا That I help أَنْ أَنْصُرَ

Light Harf

The Harf that make Fi'l Mudari light are:

حَتَّى	إِذًا	لِكَيْ	لَنْ	أَنْ
Until	In that case	So that	Will not	To

The Fi'l Mudari Chart – Lightest

ن from the normal form is dropped (compare with p. 73)

Sukoon

Lightest Harf Affectng Fil Mudari

Remain Unchanged

هُمْ If they help إِنْ يَنْصُرُوا	هُمَا If both of them help إِنْ يَنْصُرَا	هُوَ If he helps إِنْ يَنْصُرْ
هُنَّ If they (f) help إِنْ يَنْصُرْنَ	هُمَا If both of them (f) help إِنْ تَنْصُرَا	هِيَ If she helps إِنْ تَنْصُرْ
أَنْتُمْ If you all help إِنْ تَنْصُرُوا	أَنْتُمَا If both of you help إِنْ تَنْصُرَا	أَنْتَ If you help إِنْ تَنْصُرْ
أَنْتُنَّ If you all (f) help إِنْ تَنْصُرْنَ	أَنْتُمَا If both of you (f) help إِنْ تَنْصُرَا	أَنْتِ If you (f) help إِنْ تَنْصُرِي
نَحْنُ If we help إِنْ نَنْصُرْ		أَنَا If I help إِنْ أَنْصُرْ

Lightest Harf

The Harf that make Fi'l Mudari lightest are:

لِ	فَلْ	وَلْ	لَمَّا	لَمْ	إِنْ
Should	So should	And should	Not yet	Did not	If

Date: ___________________________

Lesson 1

Accompanying Video
Unit 1: 1.17.1

Learning Goals
- Know the first half of the present tense conjugations

A

Watch the accompanying video. Based on what you hear and see in the video, write/circle the correct answer.

1. In the past tense, you make changes at the end of a word, but in the present tense you make changes to the ____________________ of the word.
2. أُعَلِّمُ means '______________'.
3. يُصَلِّي means '______________'.
4. يَنْصُرُوْنَ means '____________________'.
5. If you see the letter أ at the beginning of a present tense Fi'l, it means 'I', a ن means 'we', a ي means 'he', a ي with انِ at the end means 'both of them', a ي with وْنَ at the end means '______________', and a ي with a نَ at the end means 'they (feminine)'.
6. يَدْرُسْنَ means '____________________________'.
7. If you see the letter ت at the beginning of a present tense Fi'l, it means 'you', a ت with انِ at the end means '____________________', a ت with وْنَ at the end means 'all of you', and a ت with a نَ at the end means 'all of you (feminine)'.
8. تَنْصُرانِ means '____________________________'.

Date: ______________________

B | Fill in the blanks using the word bank.

Kasrah	أَنْتُمَا	نَحْنُ	أَنْتُنَّ	أَنْتَ	هُوَ	*Present*
Past	هُمَا	هُنَّ	أَنَا	هُمْ	أَنْتُمْ	*Dhammah*

1. If a present tense Fi'l begins with an أ, the inside pronoun is ______________.

2. If a present tense Fi'l begins with a ن, the inside pronoun is ______________.

3. If a present tense Fi'l begins with a ي, the inside pronoun is ______________. If it begins with a ي and ends with انِ, the inside pronoun is ______________. If it begins with a ي and ends with ونَ, the inside pronoun is ______________. If it begins with a ي and ends with نَ, the inside pronoun is ______________.

4. If a present tense Fi'l begins with a ت, the inside pronoun is ______________. If it begins with a ت and ends with انِ, the inside pronoun is ______________. If it begins with a ت and ends with ونَ, the inside pronoun is ______________. If it begins with a ت and ends with نَ, the inside pronoun is ______________.

5. Present tense Fi'ls will begin with a fathah or a(n) ______________, but never with a(n) ______________.

6. The Fi'l نَصَرَ is ______________ tense and the Fi'l يَنْصُرُ is ______________ tense.

Date: ____________________

C

Match the Fi'l to its meaning. They have been divided up so 1-6 match with A-F, 7-12 match with G-L, and 13-15 match with M-O.

A. He teaches	1. تُعَلِّمُ
B. They help	2. يَدْرُسَانِ
C. Both of them study	3. أَدْرُسُ
D. We help	4. يَنْصُرُوْنَ
E. You teach	5. يُعَلِّمُ
F. I study	6. نَنْصُرُ

G. All of you teach	7. تَدْرُسَانِ
H. Both of you study	8. تَدْرُسُ
I. All of you (f) study	9. أَنْصُرُ
J. I help	10. يُعَلِّمْنَ
K. They (f) teach	11. تُعَلِّمُوْنَ
L. You study	12. تَدْرُسْنَ

M. All of you (f) help	13. نُعَلِّمُ
N. He studies	14. يَدْرُسُ
O. We teach	15. تَنْصُرْنَ

Date: ____________________

D

Write the present tense conjugation for يَدْرُسُ. Write the inside pronoun for each. The first one has been done as an example.

____________	____________	هُوَ يَدْرُسُ
____________	*Leave blank*	*Leave blank*
____________	____________	____________
____________	*Leave blank*	*Leave blank*
	____________	____________

Date: ______________________

E | Write the present tense conjugation for يَنْصُرُ, then translate.

هُوَ يَنْصُرُ

He helps

Leave blank *Leave blank*

Leave blank *Leave blank*

Date: ____________________

F

Identify the inside pronoun for each Fi'l.

1. تَفْعَلُ ____________
2. نَنْصُرُ ____________
3. يُؤْمِنُ ____________
4. نَجْعَلُ ____________
5. يَسْمَعُ ____________
6. نَرْزُقُ ____________
7. تُبَشِّرُ ____________
8. أَجْعَلُ ____________
9. يُنْذِرُ ____________
10. أَنْصُرُ ____________
11. يُنْزِلَانِ ____________
12. يُؤْمِنَانِ ____________
13. تُسْلِمَانِ ____________
14. تُبَشِّرُوْنَ ____________
15. يُنْذِرْنَ ____________
16. يُفْلِحُوْنَ ____________
17. تَحْسَبْنَ ____________
18. يُعَلِّمُوْنَ ____________
19. أَكْتُبُ ____________
20. تَجْعَلْنَ ____________
21. نَكْتُبُ ____________
22. يُنْزِلُ ____________
23. يَفْعَلْنَ ____________
24. تُنْذِرْنَ ____________
25. تَنْصُرَانِ ____________
26. يُسْلِمُ ____________
27. يُنْذِرَانِ ____________
28. تَكْتُبُوْنَ ____________
29. يُعَلِّمْنَ ____________
30. نَحْسَبُ ____________

Date: ____________________

G

You have learned different clues that come at the beginning and end of a present tense Fi'l. Fill in the chart with what those clues mean. Use the Fi'l يُنَزِلُ to conjugate.

If you see:	Inside pronoun	The Fi'l	The Meaning
أَ or أُ	أَنَا	أُنَزِلُ	I send down
نَ or نُ			
يَ or يُ by itself			
ي with انِ			
ي with ونَ			
ي with نَ			
تَ or تُ by itself			
ت with انِ			
ت with ونَ			
ت with نَ			

Date: ______________________

H

Circle the present tense Fi'l.

1. A. دَرَسَ
   B. دَرَسْنَ
   C. يَدْرُسُ
   D. دَرَسْنَا

2. A. نَكْسِبُ
   B. كَسَبَا
   C. كَسَبَتْ
   D. كَسَبْنَا

3. A. غَادَرَا
   B. تُغَادِرَانِ
   C. غَادَرَتَا
   D. غَادَرْتُمْ

4. A. وَجَدْنَ
   B. وَجَدْتُنَّ
   C. تَجِدْنَ
   D. وَجَدْتِ

5. A. يُسَبِّحُوْنَ
   B. سَبَّحُوْا
   C. سَبَّحَتْ
   D. سَبَّحْنَ

6. A. فَعَلْتِ
   B. يَفْعَلْنَ
   C. فَعَلْنَا
   D. فَعَلْنَ

7. A. فَتَحَتْ
   B. تَفْتَحَانِ
   C. فَتَحْنَ
   D. فَتَحُوْا

8. A. إِسْتَغْفَرَا
   B. إِسْتَغْفَرْنَ
   C. أَسْتَغْفِرُ
   D. إِسْتَغْفَرُوْا

9. A. نَشَرَ
   B. بَشَّرْنَ
   C. شَرَحْتَ
   D. يَشْرَبُ

10. A. تَخَرَّجَتَا
    B. جَلَسَتْ
    C. تَنْظُرُ
    D. رَجَعْتِ

11. A. أَفْلَحَ
    B. إِقْتَرَبَتْ
    C. أَسْمَعُ
    D. إِنْتَظَرْتُمَا

12. A. ذَهَبْنَ
    B. تَحَسَّنَ
    C. تَغَيَّرْنَا
    D. تَتَطَهَّرْنَ

Date: ____________________

Translate the Fi'ls into Arabic using the word bank.

To write	يَكْتُبُ	To warn	يُنْذِرُ	To assume	يَحْسَبُ
To hit	يَضْرِبُ	To help	يَنْصُرُ	To create	يَخْلُقُ
To teach	يُعَلِّمُ	To make	يَجْعَلُ	To look	يَنْظُرُ

1. He hits

____

2. Both of them teach

____

3. They warn

____

4. They (f) assume

____

5. You look

____

6. Both of you hit

____

7. All of you help

____

8. All of you (f) write

____

9. I create

____

10. We warn

____

Date: ____________________

Lesson 2

Accompanying Video
Unit 1: 1.17.2

Learning Goals • Memorize present tense conjugations • Identify inside pronouns in present tense Fi'ls

A

Watch the accompanying video. Based on what you hear and see in the video, write/circle the correct answer.

1. The inside pronoun of تَتَطَهَّرْنَ is ______________.

A. هُوَ *B.* هُمَا *C.* هُمْ *D.* هِيَ *E.* هُنَّ *F.* أَنْتَ *G.* أَنْتُمَا *H.* أَنْتُمْ *I.* أَنْتُنَّ *J.* أَنَا

2. The inside pronoun of تَفْهَمُونَ is ______________.

3. The inside pronoun of تُسْلِمَانِ is ______________.

4. The inside pronoun of يَشْرَبُوْنَ is ______________.

5. The inside pronoun of تَغْضَبِيْنَ is ______________.

6. The inside pronoun of أُسَاعِدُ is ______________.

7. تُنْفِقُ can mean 'you spend' or it can also mean '______________'.

8. يَسْتَغْفِرَانِ means '______________________________'.

9. تَتَعَلَّمْنَ means '______________________'.

10. تَخْرُجَانِ means '______________________'.

11. تُنْفِقِيْنَ means '______________________'.

12. تَسْتَغْفِرُوْنَ means '______________________________'.

Date: ________________

B

Fill in the blanks using the word bank.

هُوَ	هِيَ	أَنْتُنَّ	نَحْنُ	أَنْتُمَا	أَنْتِ
أَنْتُمْ	هُمْ	أَنَا	هُنَّ	هُمَا	

1. If a present tense Fi'l begins with an أ, the inside pronoun is ________________.

2. If a present tense Fi'l begins with a ن, the inside pronoun is ________________.

3. If a present tense Fi'l begins with a ي, the inside pronoun is ________________. If it begins with a ي and ends with انِ, the inside pronoun is ________________.

4. If it begins with a ي and ends with وْنَ, the inside pronoun is ________________. If it begins with a ي and ends with نَ, the inside pronoun is ________________.

5. If a present tense Fi'l begins with a ت, the inside pronoun can be أَنْتَ or ________________. If it begins with a ت and ends with ينَ, the inside pronoun is ________________. If it begins with a ت and ends with انِ, the inside pronoun can be هُمَا or ________________.

6. If it begins with a ت and ends with ونَ, the inside pronoun is ________________. If it begins with a ت and ends with نَ, the inside pronoun is ________________.

Date: ____________________

C Match the Fi'l to its meaning.

A. He writes	1. تُعَلِّمَانِ
B. Both of them help	2. تَدْرُسُ
C. They study	3. يَكْتُبُ
D. She writes	4. يَدْرُسُوْنَ
E. Both of them (f) teach	5. تَنْصُرُوْنَ
F. They (f) help	6. تَدْرُسْنَ
G. You study	7. يَنْصُرَانِ
H. Both of you write	8. أَكْتُبُ
I. All of you help	9. تَكْتُبُ
J. You (f) teach	10. نُعَلِّمُ
K. All of you (f) study	11. يَنْصُرْنَ
L. I write	12. تَكْتُبَانِ
M. We teach	13. تُعَلِّمِيْنَ

Date: ____________________

D

Write the present tense conjugation for يَسْمَعُ.

هُوَ ______	هُمَا ______	هُمْ ______
هِيَ ______	هُمَا ______	هُنَّ ______
أَنْتَ ______	أَنْتُمَا ______	أَنْتُمْ ______
أَنْتِ ______	أَنْتُمَا ______	أَنْتُنَّ ______
أَنَا ______	نَحْنُ ______	

Date: ____________________

E

Write the present tense conjugation for يَكْتُبُ, then translate.

هُوَ يَكْتُبُ

He writes

Date: ______________________

F

Identify the inside pronoun for each Fi'l, then translate the pronoun.

	Translation	Inside pronoun
1. يَكْتُبُ	He	هُوَ
2. تُحَاوِلَانِ		
3. نَلْعَبُ		
4. تَشْرَبِيْنَ		
5. يَخْرُجْنَ		
6. تَتَأَخَّرُ		
7. أَسْتَطِيْعُ		
8. تَسْتَيْقِظْنَ		
9. تَلْبَسُوْنَ		
10. يَسْتَمِعُ		

Date: ____________________

G

You have learned different clues that come at the beginning and end of a present tense Fi'l. Fill in the chart with what those clues mean. Use the Fi'l يَجْعَلُ to conjugate.

If you see:	Inside pronoun	The Fi'l	The Meaning
أَ or أُ	أَنَا	أَجْعَلُ	I make
نَ or نُ			
يَ or يُ by itself			
يـ with انِ			
يـ with وْنَ			
يـ with نَ			
تَ or تُ by itself			
تـ with انِ			
تـ with وْنَ			
تـ with نَ			
تـ with ينَ			

Date: ____________________

H Translate the Fi'ls into English using the word bank.

To write	يَكْتُبُ	To warn	يُنْذِرُ	To assume	يَحْسَبُ
To hit	يَضْرِبُ	To help	يَنْصُرُ	To create	يَخْلُقُ
To teach	يُعَلِّمُ	To make	يَجْعَلُ	To look	يَنْظُرُ

1. يَضْرِبُوْنَ ____________________
2. تَنْذُرْنَ ____________________
3. يَنْصُرَانِ ____________________
4. أَكْتُبُ ____________________
5. تَحْسَبُوْنَ ____________________
6. يَجْعَلْنَ ____________________
7. تُعَلِّمِيْنَ ____________________
8. نَنْظُرُ ____________________
9. يَخْلُقُ ____________________
10. تَكْتُبَانِ ____________________

Date: ______________________

I Translate the Fi'ls into Arabic using the word bank.

1. I make

____

2. She assumes

____

3. Both of them teach

____

4. They create

____

5. They (f) help

____

6. You hit

____

7. Both of you look

____

8. All of you look

____

9. You (f) write

____

10. All of you (f) teach

____

11. I hit

____

12. We warn

____

Date: ____________________

Lesson 3

Accompanying Video
Unit 1: 1.17.3

Learning Goals
- Practice present tense

A

Watch the accompanying video. Based on what you hear and see in the video, write/circle the correct answer.

1. يَنْصُرُ means '____________________'.
2. يُسَاعِدُوْنَ means '____________________'.
3. يَسْتَغْفِرَانِ means '____________________'.
4. يُبَشِّرْنَ means '____________________'.
5. تَتَعَلَّمْنَ means '____________________'.
6. تَحْسَبَانِ can mean '____________________', 'both of you imagine', or 'both of you (feminine) imagine'.
7. أَعْمَلُ means '____________________'.
8. تَخْرُجَانِ can have the inside pronouns ____________, أَنْتُمَا, and أَنْتُمَا.
9. تَجْعَلُ can have the inside pronouns ____________ and أَنْتِ.
10. هُمَاتُبَشِّرَانِ means '____________________'.
11. تَسْتَغْفِرُوْنَ means '____________________'.

Date: ____________________

B

Identify the inside pronoun for each Fi'l, then translate the pronoun.

	Inside pronoun	Translate
1. يَخْلُقُ	هُوَ	He
2. تَعْمَلُ		
3. أَجْمَعُ		
4. يُؤْمِنُوْنَ		
5. يُرْسِلَانِ		
6. يَرْزُقُ		
7. تَفْعَلَانِ		
8. نُنْزِلُ		
9. تَكْفُرْنَ		
10. أُنْذِرُ		

Date: ______________________

C

Identify the inside pronoun and the detail.
Hint: The attached pronoun is a detail.

	Inside pronoun	Detail
1. يَخْلُقُكُمْ	هُوَ	كُمْ
2. تَفْهَمِينَهُمْ		
3. تَحْمَدَانِهِ		
4. أُرْسِلُكُنَّ		
5. يُدَرِّسُونَكُمَا		
6. تَدْفَعُنِي		
7. تَنْصُرْنَنَا		
8. نَسْتَغْفِرُكَ		
9. يُسَاعِدَانِهِمَا		
10. تَسْمَعُوْنَهَا		

Date: ______________________

D

Identify the inside pronoun and the attached pronoun (if present), then translate them to complete the translation given.

1. ___All of you___ remember		1. تَتَذَكَّرُوْنَ
2. ________________ do wrong/injustice		2. يَظْلِمُوْنَ
3. ________________ says		3. تَقُولُ
4. ________________ fear		4. نَخَافُ
5. ________________ want		5. يُرِيدَانِ
6. ________________ work		6. أَعْمَلُ
7. ________________ assume		7. تَحْسَبَانِ
8. ________________ ask for forgiveness		8. تَسْتَغْفِرْنَ
9. ________________ congratulate		9. يُبَشِّرْنَ
10. ________________ learn		10. تَتَعَلَّمِيْنَ

Date: ____________________

11. ____We____ gather ____them____	نَحْشُرُهُمْ .11
12. ____________ returns ____________	يُعِيدُهُ .12
13. ____________ provides for ____________	يَرْزُقُكُمْ .13
14. ____________ multiplies ____________	يُضَاعِفُهَا .14
15. ____________ take ____________	تَأْخُذُوْنَهُ .15
16. ____________ inform ____________	نُنَبِّئُكُمْ .16
17. ____________ assume ____________	تَحْسَبُهُمْ .17
18. ____________ expels ____________	يُخْرِجُكُمْ .18
19. ____________ seek forgiveness from ____________	يَسْتَغْفِرُوْنَهُ .19
20. ____________ follow ____________	أَتَّبِعُكَ .20

Date: ______________________

E

Write the present tense conjugation of the Fi'l يَعْلَمُ, then translate.

		يَعْلَمُ
		He knows

Date: ____________________

F

Attach each pronoun in order to the Fi'l تَنْصُرُ, then translate.

Hint: The Fi'l doesn't change, the attached pronoun changes. So the translation will always start with 'She helps...'.

تَنْصُرُهُ

She helps him

Date: ____________

G Translate the Fi'ls into English using the word bank.

To write	يَكْتُبُ	To warn	يُنْذِرُ	To assume	يَحْسَبُ
To hit	يَضْرِبُ	To help	يَنْصُرُ	To create	يَخْلُقُ
To teach	يُعَلِّمُ	To make	يَجْعَلُ	To look	يَنْظُرُ

1. يَضْرِبُوْنَهُ

2. يَضْرِبُهُ الرَّجُلُ

3. يَضْرِبُ رَجُلاً

4. تَنْصُرُهُمْ

5. تَنْصُرُنَنِي

6. تُنْذِرُنَا

7. تُنْذِرُكُمْ الْمُسْلِمَةُ

8. تُنْذِرَانِ الْمُسْلِمَتَيْنِ

9. يُعَلِّمُ الْمُسْلِمُوْنَ

10. يُعَلِّمُوْنَ الْمُسْلِمِيْنَ

Date: ____________________

H | Translate the Fi'ls into Arabic using the word bank.

1. I help you (f)

2. She hits both of you (f)

3. Both of them teach him

4. He creates them

5. They (f) help us

6. You assume it

7. All of you warn both of them

8. We warn all of you

9. They write it

10. Both of you make it

11. You (f) teach her

12. All of you (f) warn them (f)

Date: ____________________

Lesson 4

Accompanying Video
Unit 1: 1.17.4

Learning Goals • Memorize light & lightest Harfs • Know how to make normal Fi'ls light & lightest

A

Watch the accompanying video. Based on what you hear and see in the video, write/circle the correct answer.

1. أَنْ, لَنْ, لِكَيْ, إِذًا, حَتَّى is called the ____________ group.
2. إِنْ, لَمْ, لَمَّا, وَلْ, فَلْ, لِ is called the ____________ group.
3. The light version of يَنْصُرُ is ____________.
4. The lightest version of يَنْصُرُ is ____________.
5. The light and lightest version of يَنْصُرَانِ is ____________.
6. The light and lightest version of يَنْصُرُوْنَ is ____________.
7. The light version of نَنْصُرُ is ____________.
8. The normal, light, and lightest version of يَنْصُرْنَ is ____________.
9. أَنْصُرَ is the ____________ version of أَنْصُرُ.
10. Whenever you have a word from the أَنْ, لَنْ, لِكَيْ, إِذًا, حَتَّى group, the present tense Fi'l after it becomes ____________.
11. Whenever you have a word from the إِنْ, لَمْ, لَمَّا, وَلْ, فَلْ, لِ group, the present tense Fi'l after it becomes ____________.

Date: ____________________

B

Match the normal present tense to its light version.

1. تَنْصُرَا	A. يَنْصُرُ
2. تَنْصُرْنَ	B. يَنْصُرانِ
3. تَنْصُرِيْ	C. يَنْصُرُوْنَ
4. يَنْصُرَ	D. تَنْصُرُ
5. تَنْصُرُوْا	E. تَنْصُرانِ
6. نَنْصُرَ	F. يَنْصُرْنَ
7. يَنْصُرَا	G. تَنْصُرُوْنَ
8. أَنْصُرَ	H. تَنْصُرِيْنَ
9. تَنْصُرَ	I. تَنْصُرْنَ
10. يَنْصُرُوْا	J. أَنْصُرُ
11. يَنْصُرْنَ	K. نَنْصُرُ

Date: ______________________

C | Match the normal present tense to its lightest version.

A. يَنْصُرُ	1. نَنْصُرْ
B. يَنْصُرانِ	2. يَنْصُرَا
C. يَنْصُرُوْنَ	3. أَنْصُرْ
D. تَنْصُرُ	4. تَنْصُرْنَ
E. تَنْصُرانِ	5. تَنْصُرِيْ
F. يَنْصُرْنَ	6. يَنْصُرْ
G. تَنْصُرُوْنَ	7. تَنْصُرْ
H. تَنْصُرِيْنَ	8. يَنْصُرُوْا
I. تَنْصُرْنَ	9. يَنْصُرْنَ
J. أَنْصُرُ	10. تَنْصُرَا
K. نَنْصُرُ	11. تَنْصُرُوْا

Date: ____________________

D

Circle the light Harf, then write the light Harfs in order.

1. A. فِي
   B. أَنْ
   C. إِنَّ

4. A. أَنْ
   B. إِلَى
   C. مِنْ

7. A. لَمْ
   B. لِكَيْ
   C. قَبْلَ

2. A. بَيْنَ
   B. عَلَى
   C. لِكَيْ

5. A. لَكِنَّ
   B. إِذًا
   C. لَمْ

8. A. حَتَّى
   B. إِلَى
   C. أَنَّ

3. A. إِنْ
   B. لَنْ
   C. عَنْ

6. A. فَلْ
   B. لَعَلَّ
   C. حَتَّى

9. A. وَلْ
   B. خَلْفَ
   C. لَنْ

Write the light harfs in order:

________ ________ ________ ________ ________

Date: ____________________

E Circle the lightest Harf, then write the lightest Harfs in order.

1. A. إِلَى
   B. أَنَّ
   C. إِنْ

2. A. لِكَيْ
   B. وَلْ
   C. فَوْقَ

3. A. لِ
   B. لَنْ
   C. إِلَى

4. A. وَ
   B. كَأَنَّ
   C. لَمَّا

5. A. تَ
   B. عَنْ
   C. لَمْ

6. A. حَتَّى
   B. عَلَى
   C. إِنْ

7. A. إِنَّ
   B. فَلْ
   C. بَعْدَ

8. A. لَنْ
   B. أَنَّ
   C. لِ

9. A. لَمْ
   B. مِنْ
   C. عَنْ

Write the lightest harfs in order:

__________ __________ __________ __________ __________ __________

Date: ____________________

F

Write the light version of the present tense conjugation for يَدْرُسُ along with a light harf of your choice.

Date: ____________________

G

Write the lightest version of the present tense conjugation for يَدْرُسُ along with a lightest harf of your choice.

Date: ______________________

H

Label each Fi'l as Normal (N), Light (L1), or Lightest (L2). If it can be more than one, write all that apply.

1. تَفْعَلُ ______________
2. نَنْصُرَ ______________
3. يُؤْمِنْ ______________
4. نَجْعَلُ ______________
5. يَسْمَعُ ______________
6. نَرْزُقَ ______________
7. تُبَشِّرْ ______________
8. أَجْعَلْ ______________
9. يُنْذِرَ ______________
10. أَنْصُرَ ______________
11. يُنْزِلَانِ ______________
12. يُؤْمِنَا ______________
13. تُسْلِمَا ______________
14. تُبَشِّرُوْا ______________
15. يُنْذِرْنَ ______________
16. يُفْلِحُوْا ______________
17. تَحْسَبْنَ ______________
18. يُعَلِّمُوْنَ ______________
19. يَكْتُبَا ______________
20. تَجْعَلْنَ ______________
21. نَكْتُبَ ______________
22. يُنْزِلْ ______________
23. يُؤْمِنُوْا ______________
24. تُنْذِرْنَ ______________
25. أَنْصُرْ ______________
26. يُسْلِمَ ______________
27. يُنْذِرَا ______________
28. يَكْتُبُوْا ______________
29. يُعَلِّمْنَ ______________
30. تَحْسَبْ ______________

Date: ____________________

Lesson 5

Accompanying Video
Unit 1: 1.17.5

Learning Goals
- Identify light and lightest words

A

Watch the accompanying video. Based on what you hear and see in the video, write/circle the correct answer.

1. لَمْ means '________________'. لَمْ is a crazy word because it only comes with the present tense and when it does, it forces the meaning to be negative and in the past.
2. لَمْ يَنْصُرْ means '________________________'.
3. لَنْ means '________________'. This crazy word takes a present tense Fi'l and makes the meaning negative and in the future.
4. لَنْ تُنْفِقَ means '________________________' (give one answer).
5. لَمَّا means '________________'.
6. لَمَّا يَدْخُلْ means '________________________'.
7. إِنْ means '________________'.
8. أَنْ means '________________'.
9. أَنْ يُبَشِّرْنَ means '________________________'.
10. حَتّٰى means '________________'.
11. حَتّٰى تَحْسَبَا means '________________________________' (give one answer).

Date: ________________

B | Fill in the blanks using the word bank.

Past *Sukoon* *Fathah* *Light* *Lightest* *Same* *Present*

لَنْ لَمْ حَتَّى

1. ______________ tense Fi'ls can have three different versions: normal, light, and lightest.

   ______________ tense Fi'ls can have only one version.

2. Light Harfs make the present tense Fi'ls after them ______________. Lightest Harfs make the present tense Fi'ls after them ______________.

3. To make a word light, you change the dhammah at the end of the word into a(n) ______________ or take off the ن.

4. To make a word lightest, you change the dhammah at the end of the word into a(n) ______________ or take off the ن.

5. The normal, light, and lightest versions are the ______________ for هُنَّ and أَنْتُنَّ.

6. ______________ is a lightest Harf that means 'did not'. It is a crazy Harf that comes with the present tense, but the meaning is in the past tense.

7. ______________ is a light Harf that means 'will not'.

8. ______________ is a light Harf that means 'until'.

Date: ____________________

C

Match each Harf to its meaning, then put the Fi'l in the box in their correct category.

A. Will not	1. حَتَّى
B. Not yet	2. أَنْ
C. To	3. إِنْ
D. Did not	4. لَمَّا
E. Until	5. لَنْ
F. If	6. لَمْ

لَمَّا　　أَنْ　　إِنْ　　حَتَّى　　لَمْ　　لَنْ

Light Harf:

____

____

____

Lightest Harf:

____

____

____

Date: ____________________

D

Write the correct present tense conjugation of the Fi'l يَعْلَمُ with the harf لَنْ, then translate.

		لَنْ يَعْلَمَ
		He will not know
	لَنْ تَعْلَمَا	
	Both of you will not know	

Date: ______________________

E

Write the correct present tense conjugation of the Fi'l يَعْلَمُ with the harf لَمْ, then translate.

لَمْ يَعْلَمْ

He did not know

لَمْ تَعْلَمَا

Both of you did not know

Date: ____________________

F

Translate the Fi'ls into English using the word bank.

To write	يَكْتُبُ	To warn	يُنْذِرُ	To assume	يَحْسَبُ
To hit	يَضْرِبُ	To help	يَنْصُرُ	To create	يَخْلُقُ
To teach	يُعَلِّمُ	To make	يَجْعَلُ	To look at	يَنْظُرُ

1. يَضْرِبُ

____

2. لَمْ يَضْرِبْ

____

3. لَنْ يَضْرِبُوْا

____

4. إِنْ تَضْرِبْهُمْ

____

5. لَمَّا تُنْذِرْنَ

____

6. أَنْ تُنْذِرُوْا

____

7. لَنْ تُنْذِرِيْهَا

____

8. لَمْ أَكْتُبْ

____

9. أَنْ يَكْتُبَ

____

10. حَتَّى نَكْتُبَهُ

____

Date: ____________________

G | Translate the Fi'ls into Arabic using the word bank.

1. We help

____

2. We help them

____

3. Until we help

____

4. Until we help them

____

5. They teach

____

6. If they teach

____

7. If they teach both of you

____

8. I make

____

9. I make it

____

10. I did not make it

____

11. I have not made it yet

____

12. I will not make it

____

Date: ______________________

H | Complete the translation given.

1. You/she did not know	لَمْ تَعْلَمْ .1
2. ______________ study	حَتَّى يَدْرُسُوا .2
3. ______________ eat	إِنْ تَأْكُلِيْ .3
4. ______________ go	أَنْ نَذْهَبَ .4
5. ______________ help ______________	لَنْ يُسَاعِدْنَهَا .5
6. ______________ warned ______________	لَمَّا أُنْذِرَ .6
7. ______________ teach ______________	لَمْ تُعَلِّمْهُمْ .7
8. ______________ ask ______________	إِنْ تَسْأَلْنَا .8
9. ______________ teach ______________	لَنْ تُدَرِّسُوْنِيْ .9
10. ______________ understand ______________	أَنْ يَفْقَهُوْهُ .10

Date: ______________________________

Lesson 6

Accompanying Video
Unit 1: 1.17.6

Learning Goals

- Know the meanings of all light and lightest Harfs

A

Watch the accompanying video. Based on what you hear and see in the video, write/circle the correct answer.

1. لَمَّا تُسَاعِدَا means '______________________________' (give one answer).

2. إِنْ يَسْتَغْفِرَا means '______________________________'.

3. لِكَيْ means '______________'.

4. لِكَيْ تَسْتَنِدُوْا means '______________________________'.

5. لِ means '______________'.

6. لِتَتَعَلَّمْنَ means '______________________________'.

7. لِكَيْ can be said in three ways: لِ, ______________, and لِكَيْ, but they all mean the same thing. Now there are two of لِ, one from the light family and one from the lightest.

8. فَ means 'so' and وَ means 'and', the لْ part means '______________'.

9. إِذًا means '______________'.

10. إِذًا تُنْفِقِيْ means '______________________________'.

11. كَيْ تَجْعَلَ means '______________________________' (give one answer).

12. لِتَعْمَلْنَ means '______________________________'.

Date: ______________________

B

Match each Harf to its meaning, then write out all the light and lightest Harfs.

A. So...should	1. لِكَيْ
B. Should	2. وَلْ
C. And...should	3. لِ
D. So that	4. فَلْ
E. In that case	5. إذاً

Write the light Harfs in order:

________ ________ ________ ________ ________

Write the lightest Harfs in order:

________ ________ ________ ________ ________ ________

لِكَيْ has three versions:

________ ________ ________

Date: ______________________

C

Identify the inside pronoun for each Fi'l, then translate each pronoun and Harf.

Translate the Harf	Translate the inside pronoun	Inside pronoun	
Until	He	هُوَ	1. حَتّٰى يَخْلُقَ
			2. إِذًا تَعْمَلِي
			3. لِكَيْ أَجْمَعَ
			4. فَلْيُؤْمِنُوا
			5. إِنْ تَخْرُجْنَ
			6. لَنْ يَرْزُقَا
			7. لَمْ نَفْعَلْ
			8. وَلْيَخْرُجْ
			9. لِتَنْصُرَ
			10. لِتَكْتُبَ

Date: ____________________

D

Identify the inside pronoun and the attached pronoun, then translate it to complete the translation given.

1.	If all of you ______ do	1. إِنْ تَفْعَلُوْا
2.	____________ make	2. لَمْ نَجْعَلْ
3.	____________ succeed	3. لَنْ تُفْلِحُوْا
4.	____________ reach	4. أَنْ يَبْلُغَا
5.	____________ know	5. حَتَّى نَعْلَمَ
6.	____________ worship	6. فَلْيَعْبُدُوْا
7.	____________ drown	7. لِتُغْرِقَ
8.	____________ entered ____________	8. لَمَّا يَدْخُلْ
9.	____________ be careful	9. وَلْيَتَلَطَّفْ
10.	____________ associate	10. لَمْ أُشْرِكْ

Date: ____________________

11. ______________ be able to	11. لَنْ تَسْتَطِيعَ
12. ______________ want	12. إِنْ يُرِيدَا
13. ______________ believe	13. وَلْيُؤْمِنُوا
14. ______________ look	14. فَلْيَنْظُرْ
15. ______________ come to ______________	15. إِنْ يَأْتُوكُمْ
16. ______________ test ______________	16. لِنَبْلُوَهُمْ
17. ______________ be hospitable to ______________	17. أَنْ يُضَيِّفُوهُمَا
18. ______________ comes to ______________	18. حَتَّى يَأْتِيَنَا
19. ______________ find ______________	19. لَمْ يَجِدْكَ
20. ______________ helps ______________	20. إِنْ يَنْصُرْكُمُ اللَّهُ

Date: ______________________

E

Translate the Fi'ls into English using the word bank.

To write	يَكْتُبُ	To warn	يُنْذِرُ	To assume	يَحْسَبُ
To hit	يَضْرِبُ	To help	يَنْصُرُ	To create	يَخْلُقُ
To teach	يُعَلِّمُ	To make	يَجْعَلُ	To look	يَنْظُرُ

1. لَمْ أَضْرِبْ
____

2. لَمْ أَضْرِبْهُمْ
____

3. لِكَيْ تَجْعَلَ
____

4. كَيْ تَجْعَلِيْهِ
____

5. لِنَجْعَلَهُ
____

6. فَلْيُعَلِّمَا
____

7. وَلْيُعَلِّمُوْهُمَا
____

8. لِيُعَلِّمْكُمَا
____

9. لِيُنْذِرْ
____

10. إِذًا تَكْتُبَ
____

Date: ____________________

F | Translate the Fi'ls into Arabic using the word bank.

1. He helps

2. He should help us

3. And he should help both of them

4. So he should help you

5. In that case we will write

6. We did not write it

7. We have not written it yet

8. We will not write it

9. So that all of you teach me

10. If all of you (f) teach her

11. To teach (all of you) him

12. Until I teach you (f)

Date: ____________________

Qur’anic Application

Label the highlighted word as past tense Fi’l, present tense Fi’l, Faa’il, or Maf’ool.

تَبَارَكَ الَّذِي بِيَدِهِ الْمُلْكُ وَهُوَ عَلَىٰ كُلِّ شَيْءٍ قَدِيرٌ ﴿١﴾ الَّذِي خَلَقَ الْمَوْتَ وَالْحَيَاةَ

لِيَبْلُوَكُمْ أَيُّكُمْ أَحْسَنُ عَمَلًا ۚ وَهُوَ الْعَزِيزُ الْغَفُورُ ﴿٢﴾ الَّذِي خَلَقَ سَبْعَ

سَمَاوَاتٍ طِبَاقًا ۖ مَّا تَرَىٰ فِي خَلْقِ الرَّحْمَٰنِ مِن تَفَاوُتٍ ۖ فَارْجِعِ الْبَصَرَ هَلْ تَرَىٰ مِن

فُطُورٍ ﴿٣﴾ ثُمَّ ارْجِعِ الْبَصَرَ كَرَّتَيْنِ يَنقَلِبْ إِلَيْكَ الْبَصَرُ خَاسِئًا وَهُوَ حَسِيرٌ ﴿٤﴾

وَلَقَدْ زَيَّنَّا السَّمَاءَ الدُّنْيَا بِمَصَابِيحَ وَجَعَلْنَاهَا رُجُومًا لِّلشَّيَاطِينِ ۖ وَأَعْتَدْنَا لَهُمْ

عَذَابَ السَّعِيرِ ﴿٥﴾ وَلِلَّذِينَ كَفَرُوا بِرَبِّهِمْ عَذَابُ جَهَنَّمَ ۖ وَبِئْسَ الْمَصِيرُ ﴿٦﴾

CHAPTER 4
Forbidding

Chapter 4

Now that we have completed our study of the Fi'l Mudari, we can learn its two derivative forms: الفِعْلُ الأَمْرُ (command verb) and الفِعْلُ النَّهِي (forbidding verb). There are five observations we can make about these verbs:

1. You cannot command in the past tense. It does not make sense to say 'Don't ate that!'
2. You cannot command someone who is not there. You cannot command the following inside pronouns: هُوَ, هُمَا, هُمْ, هِيَ, هُمَا, هُنَّ.
3. You cannot command yourself. You cannot command the following inside pronouns: أَنَا and نَحْنُ. Since you cannot command in the first person and in the third person, you can only command in the second person: أَنْتَ, أَنْتُمَا, أَنْتُمْ, أَنْتِ, أَنْتُمَا, أَنْتُنَّ.
4. Forbidding is easier than commanding.
5. Commanding doesn't always mean commanding. It can be a suggestion, advice, dua, permission or request

Rules for Forbidding

1. Put the Fi'l Mudari in second person.
2. Make it lightest.
3. Put لا in front of it.

Application

Don't help!

1. Fi'l Mudari 2nd person: تَنْصُرُ
2. Lightest: تَنْصُرْ
3. Put لا before it: لاتَنْصُرْ

Don't help (f)!

1. Fi'l Mudari 2nd person: تَنْصُرِينَ
2. Lightest: تَنْصُرِي

3. Put لا before it: لاتَنْصُرِي

Don't you all help!

1. Fi'l Mudari 2nd person: تَنْصُرُونَ
2. Lightest: تَنْصُرُوا
3. Put لا before it: لاتَنْصُرُوا

Difference between Negating and Forbidding

It is important to note the difference between forbidding and negating. For example, a friend may say, "I noticed you don't write." In this case, "you don't write" is a negation, not forbidding. Negating is an observation. When negating, we use a لا as well but it does not affect the Fi'l in any way:

Lightest = forbidding → لَاتَنْصُرْ

You, don't help!

Normal = negating → لَاتَنْصُرُ

You don't help.

Notice that the Fi'l in negation is normal, whereas in forbidding it is lightest.

Date: ______________________

Lesson 1

Accompanying Video
Unit 1: 1.18.1

Learning Goals

- Know how to turn a present tense into its forbidding form

A

Watch the accompanying video. Based on what you hear and see in the video, write/ circle the correct answer.

1. When somebody tells you not to do something, they are ____________________ you.

2. When somebody tells you to do something, they are ____________________ you.

3. When commanding or forbidding, you can't do either in the _______________ tense.

4. You can't command or forbid for _______________-person pronouns like هُوَ, هُمَا, or هُمْ.

5. You can't command or forbid _______________.

6. Commanding doesn't always mean _______________, a command can be a permission sometimes, it can be advice sometimes, it can actually be a command sometimes, or it can be a dua' sometimes.

7. To forbid, you have to put the word لَا in front a present tense Fi'l and turn the Fi'l into its _______________ form.

8. لَا تَنْصُرْ means '____________________'.

9. لَا تَنْصُرِ means '____________________'.

10. The way to write لَا تَدْرُسُوْنَ in its forbidding form is ____________________.

Date: ____________________

B | Fill in the blanks using the word bank.

Is not	*Don't help!*	*Comment*	*Is*	*You don't help*	*Present*
Forbidding	أَنْتَ	أَنْتُمَا	أَنْتِ	أَنْتُمْ	أَنْتُنَّ *Commanding*

1. You can only command and forbid in the ______________ tense.

2. You can't command or forbid yourself or someone who isn't there. 'They should help' is just a(n) ______________, not a command.

3. You can only command someone who is there, so the pronouns you can command are: ___________, ___________, ___________, ___________, and ___________.

4. ______________ is easier than ______________.

5. لَا plus a normal present tense Fi'l like لَاتَنْصُرُ ______________ a command and means '______________'.

6. لَا plus a lightest present tense Fi'l like لَاتَنْصُرْ ______________ a command and means '______________'.

Date: ______________________

C | Match the Fi'l to its meaning.

A. She doesn't help	1. لَا تَنْصُرِيْ
B. You, don't help!	2. لَا تَنْصُرَا
C. You (f), don't help!	3. لَا تَنْصُرُ
D. All of you, don't help!	4. لَا تَنْصُرُوْا
E. Both of you, don't help!	5. لَا تَنْصُرْ
F. All of you (f), don't help!	6. لَا تَنْصُرْنَ

D | Write the forbidding forms for يَنْصُرُ, then translate.

لَاتَنْصُرْ

You, don't help!

Date: ____________________

E

Identify if the Fi'l is forbidding or negating. Also, identify the inside pronoun.

	Yes/No	Inside pronoun
1. لَا تَكْتُبْ	Yes	أَنْتَ
2. لَا يَنْصُرُوْنَ	______	______
3. لَا تَلْعَبِيْ	______	______
4. لَا تَشْرَبَا	______	______
5. لَا أَشْرَبُ	______	______
6. لَا تَحْزَنْ	______	______
7. لَا تُغَادِرُوْا	______	______
8. لَا تُفْلِحِيْنَ	______	______
9. لَا تُدَرِّسْ	______	______
10. لَا تَفْعَلْنَ	______	______

Date: ________________

F

Identify the inside pronoun and the attached pronoun, then translate it to complete the translation given.

1. Both of you, ______, don't say! — ١. لَا تَقُولَا
2. ______________, don't assume! — ٢. لَا تَحْسَبِيْ
3. ______________, don't leave! — ٣. لَا تَخْرُجَا
4. ______________, don't send down! — ٤. لَا تُنْزِلْ
5. ______________, don't warn! — ٥. لَا تُنْذِرَا
6. ______________, don't work! — ٦. لَا تَعْمَلِيْ
7. ______________, don't make! — ٧. لَا تَجْعَلُوْا
8. ______________, don't congratulate! — ٨. لَا تُبَشِّرَا
9. ______________, don't take! — ٩. لَا تَتَّخِذُوْا
10. ______________, don't write! — ١٠. لَا تَكْتُبْ

Date: ______________________

G

Translate the Fi'ls into English using the word bank.

To write	يَكْتُبُ	To warn	يُنْذِرُ	To assume	يَحْسَبُ
To hit	يَضْرِبُ	To help	يَنْصُرُ	To create	يَخْلُقُ
To teach	يُعَلِّمُ	To make	يَجْعَلُ	To look	يَنْظُرُ

1. تَجْعَلُوْنَ

____

2. لَا تَجْعَلُوْنَ

____

3. لَا تَجْعَلُوْا

____

4. لَا يَحْسَبَانِ

____

5. لَا تَحْسَبَانِ

____

6. لَا تَحْسَبَا

____

7. لَا تَخْلُقُوْنَ

____

8. لَا تَضْرِبِيْ

____

9. لَا تُنْذِرُ

____

10. لَا تَنْظُرِيْ

____

Date: ____________________

H

Translate the Fi'ls into Arabic using the word bank.

1. I assume

____

2. You (f) assume

____

3. You (f) don't assume

____

4. You (f), don't assume!

____

5. They don't hit

____

6. All of you don't hit

____

7. All of you, don't hit!

____

8. We don't help

____

9. You, don't write!

____

10. All of you don't teach

____

11. Both of you, don't make!

____

12. You (f), don't look!

____

Date: ______________________

Qur'anic Application

Label the highlighted word as past tense Fi'l, present tense Fi'l, forbidding, Faa'il, or Maf'ool.

تَبَارَكَ الَّذِي بِيَدِهِ الْمُلْكُ وَهُوَ عَلَىٰ كُلِّ شَيْءٍ قَدِيرٌ ﴿١﴾ الَّذِي خَلَقَ الْمَوْتَ وَالْحَيَاةَ

لِيَبْلُوَكُمْ أَيُّكُمْ أَحْسَنُ عَمَلًا ۚ وَهُوَ الْعَزِيزُ الْغَفُورُ ﴿٢﴾ الَّذِي خَلَقَ سَبْعَ

سَمَاوَاتٍ طِبَاقًا ۖ مَّا تَرَىٰ فِي خَلْقِ الرَّحْمَٰنِ مِن تَفَاوُتٍ ۖ فَارْجِعِ الْبَصَرَ هَلْ تَرَىٰ مِن

فُطُورٍ ﴿٣﴾ ثُمَّ ارْجِعِ الْبَصَرَ كَرَّتَيْنِ يَنقَلِبْ إِلَيْكَ الْبَصَرُ خَاسِئًا وَهُوَ حَسِيرٌ ﴿٤﴾

وَلَقَدْ زَيَّنَّا السَّمَاءَ الدُّنْيَا بِمَصَابِيحَ وَجَعَلْنَاهَا رُجُومًا لِّلشَّيَاطِينِ ۖ وَأَعْتَدْنَا لَهُمْ

عَذَابَ السَّعِيرِ ﴿٥﴾ وَلِلَّذِينَ كَفَرُوا بِرَبِّهِمْ عَذَابُ جَهَنَّمَ ۖ وَبِئْسَ الْمَصِيرُ ﴿٦﴾

CHAPTER 5
Commanding

Chapter 5

Recall that there were two derivative forms of the Fi'l Mudari: الفِعلُ الأَمْرُ (command verb) and الفِعلُ النَّهيُ (forbidding verb). We learned about forbidding in the previous chapter; this chapter we will learn about commanding.

Rules for Commanding

1. Put the Fi'l Mudari in second person.
2. Make it lightest.
3. Get rid of ت from the beginning.
4. If the beginning letter has a Sukoon on it, then you can't read it. Add an Alif to solve this problem.
5. If the second to last letter (from step 1) has Dhamma, put a Dhamma on the Alif, otherwise put Kasrah.

Application

Help!

1. Fi'l Mudari 2nd person: تَنْصُرُ
2. Lightest: تَنْصُرْ
3. Remove ت from beginning: نْصُرْ
4. Sukoon on first letter, so add ا in the beginning: انْصُرْ
5. 2nd last letter in step 1 has Dhamma, so put Dhamma: اُنْصُرْ

Help (f)!

1. Fi'l Mudari 2nd person: تَنْصُرِينَ
2. Lightest: تَنْصُرِي
3. Remove ت from beginning: نْصُرِي
4. Sukoon on first letter, so add ا in the beginning: انْصُرِي

5. 2nd last letter in step 1 has Dhamma, so put Dhamma: أُنْصُرِي

Listen!

1. Fi'l Mudari 2nd person: تَسْمَعُ
2. Lightest: تَسْمَعْ
3. Remove ت from beginning: سْمَعْ
4. Sukoon on first letter, so add ا in the beginning: اسْمَعْ
5. 2nd last letter in step 1 does not have Dhamma, so put Kasra: إِسْمَعْ

You all teach!

1. Fi'l Mudari 2nd person: تُعَلِّمُونَ
2. Lightest: تُعَلِّمُوا
3. Remove ت from beginning: عَلِّمُوا
4. Not a sukoon on first letter, so no need to add ا or do step 5: عَلِّمُوا

Date: ______________________

Lesson 1

Accompanying Video
Unit 1: 1.19.1

Learning Goals
- Know how to turn a present tense Fi'l into a command

A

Watch the accompanying video. Based on what you hear and see in the video, write/circle the correct answer.

1. When turning present tense Fi'ls into commands, there are two steps involved and sometimes three. The first step is to make the Fi'l into its ______________ form.

2. Step two is to get rid of the ______________.

3. If after the second step you can read the word normally, you are done forming the command. If you can't read the word normally and the first letter has a(n) ______________ on it, then a third step is required.

4. The third step is to add a(n) ______________ before the word. To figure out which harakah goes on top of the ا, look at the letter right after the letter with the sukoon. If that letter has a dhammah (ُ) on it, then put a dhammah on the ا. If it has a fathah (َ) or kasrah (ِ), put a kasrah on the ا (note that this is different from the way Ustadh Nouman taught in the video, but it is an easier way to find which letter to look for).

5. The command form of تَتَنَزَّلُ is ______________.

6. The command form of تَقْتَرِبُ is ______________.

Date: ____________________

B | Fill in the blanks using the work bank.

Command	*Lightest*	*Forbid*	*Three*	*Present*

أَنْتُنَّ   ت   أَنْتُمْ   أَنْتِ   ا   أَنْتُمَا   أَنْتَ

1. The formula to ______________ someone in Arabic is: لَا + the lightest present tense.

2. You can only turn a(n) ______________ tense Fi'l into a command.

3. You can only forbid or command someone who is there, so the pronouns you can forbid or command are: ___________, ___________, ___________, ___________, and ___________.

4. There are sometimes two and sometimes ______________ steps to turn a present tense into a ______________. First, make it ___________. Then, take the ___________ off from the beginning of the word. If the word is readable, then you're done, but if the word is unreadable, you add a(n) ___________.

Date: ____________________

C Match each Fi'l to its meaning.

A. You help	1. أُنْصُرْ
B. You, help!	2. أُنْصُرُوا
C. You (f), help!	3. أُنْصُرَا
D. All of you, help!	4. أُنْصُرِي
E. Both of you, help!	5. تَنْصُرُ
F. All of you (f), help!	6. أُنْصُرْنَ

D Write the commanding forms of يَكْتُبُ in order, then translate.

أُكْتُبْ

You, write!

Date: ____________________

E

Identify the second to last letter of each present tense Fi'l, then identify if the Fi'l is normal, light, or lightest. If it can be more than one, write all that apply.
Hint: The second last letter is also the letter right after the letter with the sukoon.

1. تَكْتُبُ ______ت______ ______Normal______

2. يَنْصُرُوْنَ ____________ ____________

3. تَلْعَبِيْ ____________ ____________

4. تَشْرَبَانِ ____________ ____________

5. تَلْعَبُوْنَ ____________ ____________

6. نَأْكُلُ ____________ ____________

7. تَشْرَبْ ____________ ____________

8. يَذْهَبَا ____________ ____________

9. تَسْمَعُوْا ____________ ____________

10. تَرْجِعِيْنَ ____________ ____________

Date: ______________________

F

Go through the steps to turn each of the following present tense Fi'ls into commands. Remember, not all Fi'ls will have step 3/4.

Step 3/4	Step 2	Step 1	
اُكْتُبْ	كْتُبْ	تَكْتُبْ	1. تَكْتُبُ
			2. تَنْصُرُوْنَ
			3. تَلْعَبِيْنَ
			4. تُذَكِّرُ
			5. تَشْرَبَانِ
			6. تُغَادِرْنَ
			7. تَرْجِعِيْنَ
			8. تَسْجُدَانِ
			9. تَكْرُمْنَ
			10. تَقْرَأُ

Date: ____________________

G Translate the following Fi'ls into English using the word bank.

To write	يَكْتُبُ	To warn	يُنْذِرُ	To assume	يَحْسَبُ
To hit	يَضْرِبُ	To help	يَنْصُرُ	To create	يَخْلُقُ
To teach	يُعَلِّمُ	To make	يَجْعَلُ	To look	يَنْظُرُ

1. اِجْعَلْ
____

2. اِجْعَلُوْا
____

3. لَا تَجْعَلُوْا
____

4. اُنْصُرْ
____

5. اُنْصُرِيْ
____

6. اِضْرِبْ
____

7. اِضْرِبَا
____

8. لَا تَضْرِبَا
____

9. عَلِّمْ
____

10. عَلِّمُوْهُ
____

Date: ______________________

H | Translate the following Fi'ls into Arabic using the word bank.

1. You write

____

2. You (f) write

____

3. You (f) don't assume

____

4. You (f), write!

____

5. You (f), don't write!

____

6. All of you, look!

____

7. Both of you, don't look!

____

8. Both of you, teach!

____

9. Both of you (f), teach!

____

10. All of you (f), teach!

____

11. You, hit him!

____

12. All of you (f), don't hit!

____

Date: ______________________

I

Translate each of the following into English with the help of the definitions given.

		Translation	
1.	اِجْعَلْ	______________________	Make: يَجْعَلُ
2.	اُدْرُسِيْ	______________________	Study: يَدْرُسُ
3.	لَا تَعْمَلَا	______________________	Work: يَعْمَلُ
4.	اُسْجُدُوْا	______________________	Prostrate: يَسْجُدُ
5.	لَا تَأْخُذْ	______________________	Take: يَأْخُذُ
6.	لَا تُعَلِّمُوْا	______________________	Teach: يُعَلِّمُ
7.	اُنْصُرْنَ	______________________	Help: يَنْصُرُ
8.	اِشْرَبْ	______________________	Drink: يَشْرَبُ
9.	لَا تَنْظُرْ	______________________	Look: يَنْظُرُ
10.	اِقْرَئِيْ	______________________	Read: يَقْرَأُ

Date: ______________________

Translation

11. لَا تَكْتُبْنَ	______________________	Write: يَكْتُبُ
12. اِنْتَظِرُوْا	______________________	Wait: يَنْتَظِرُ
13. اُخْرُجْ	______________________	Leave: يَخْرُجُ
14. لَا تَضْرِبَا	______________________	Hit: يَضْرِبُ
15. لَا تَأْكُلِيْ	______________________	Eat: يَأْكُلُ
16. اِذْهَبْ	______________________	Go: يَذْهَبُ
17. لَا تَلْعَبُوْا	______________________	Play: يَلْعَبُ
18. بَشِّرْنَ	______________________	Congratulate: يُبَشِّرُ
19. اُذْكُرِيْ	______________________	Mention: يَذْكُرُ
20. لَا تَقْلَقْ	______________________	Worry: يَقْلَقُ

Date: ______________________

Lesson 2

Accompanying Video
Unit 1: 1.19.2

Learning Goals
- Practice commanding and forbidding

A

Watch the accompanying video. Based on what you hear and see in the video, write/ circle the correct answer.

1. The command form of تَذْهَبَانِ is ____________________.
   A. تَذْهَبَا *B.* اِذْهَبَانْ *C.* اِذْهَبَا *D.* اُذْهَبَا

2. The forbidding form of تَسْأَلَنِهُمَا is ____________________.
   A. لَا تَسْأَلَنِهِمَا *B.* لَا تَسْأَلْهُمَا *C.* لَا اِسْأَلَنِهِمَا *D.* لَا اِسْأَلْهُمَا

3. The commanding form of تَكْتُبُ كِتَابَيْنِ is ____________________.
   A. اِكْتُبْ كِتَابَيْنِ *B.* تَكْتُبْ كِتَابَيْنِ *C.* تُكْتُبْ كِتَابَيْنِ *D.* اُكْتُبْ كِتَابَيْنِ

4. The commanding form of تَتَكَلَّمِينَ الْعَرَبِيَّةَ is ____________________.
   A. كَلَّمِي الْعَرَبِيَّةَ *B.* كَلَّمِينَ الْعَرَبِيَّةَ *C.* تَكَلَّمِي الْعَرَبِيَّةَ *D.* تَكَلَّمِينَ الْعَرَبِيَّةَ

5. The forbidding form of تَكْتُبُونَ عَلَيْهَا is ____________________.
   A. لَا اَكْتُبُوا عَلَيْهَا *B.* لَا اُكْتُبُوا عَلَيْهَا *C.* لَا تَكْتُبُوا عَلَيْهَا *D.* لَا تَكْتُبُونَ عَلَيْهَا

6. The forbidding form of تَذْهَبُ إِلَى الْبَيْتِ is ____________________.
   A. لَا تَذْهَبْ إِلَى الْبَيْتِ *B.* لَا اِذْهَبْ إِلَى الْبَيْتِ *C.* لَا اُذْهَبْ إِلَى الْبَيْتِ *D.* لَا تَذْهَبُ إِلَى الْبَيْتِ

7. The command form of تَقُولُونَ شَيْءً is ____________________.
   A. اِقُولُوا شَيْءً *B.* اُقُولُوا شَيْءً *C.* قُولُونَ شَيْءً *D.* قُولُوا شَيْءً

8. The forbidding form of تُبَشِّرُهُمْ is ____________________.
   A. لَا اُبَشِّرْهُمْ *B.* لَا اِبَشِّرْهُمْ *C.* لَا تُبَشِّرْهُمْ *D.* لَا بَشِّرْهُمْ

Date: ______________________

B | Write the forbidding forms for يَدْرُسُ, then translate.

You, don't study!

C | Write the commanding forms for يَدْرُسُ, then translate.

Date: ____________________

D

Identify the inside pronoun and the detail for each of the following Fi'ls, then identify the second to last letter of each Fi'l (if there is one).

2nd last letter	Detail	Inside pronoun	
ت	هُ	أَنْتَ	1. أُكْتُبْهُ
			2. لَا تَنْصُرُوْهَا
			3. أُكْتُبْ كِتَاباً
			4. اُنْصُرِيْ المُعَلِّمَ
			5. لَا تَتَكَلَّمْ العَرَبِيَّةَ
			6. دَرِّسُوْا الطُّلَّابَ
			7. أُتْرُكْنِيْ
			8. لَا تَأْخُذَا السَّيَّارَةَ
			9. أُشْكُرِيْهِنَّ
			10. اِنْتَظِرْنَنَا

Date: ____________________

E Translate the following Fi'ls into English using the word bank.

To write	يَكْتُبُ	To warn	يُنْذِرُ	To assume	يَحْسَبُ
To hit	يَضْرِبُ	To help	يَنْصُرُ	To create	يَخْلُقُ
To teach	يُعَلِّمُ	To make	يَجْعَلُ	To look	يَنْظُرُ

1. اِجْعَلْ

____

2. اِجْعَلْهَا

____

3. لَا تَجْعَلْ

____

4. لَا تَجْعَلْهَا

____

5. اِضْرِبِي

____

6. اِضْرِبِيْهِمْ

____

7. لَا تَضْرِبَا

____

8. لَا تَضْرِبَاهُمَا

____

9. أُنْظُرْ

____

10. لَا تَنْظُرُوْا

____

Date: ____________________

F | Translate the following Fi'ls into Arabic using the word bank.

1. You help her

____

2. You, help her!

____

3. I don't help her

____

4. You, don't help her!

____

5. All of you (f) teach them

____

6. All of you (f), teach them!

____

7. All of you (f) don't teach them

____

8. All of you (f), don't teach them!

____

9. Both of you write a book

____

10. Both of you, write a book!

____

11. Both of you don't write a book

____

12. Both of you, don't write a book!

____

Date: ____________________

Qur'anic Application

Label each highlighted Fi'l below as past tense, present tense, forbidding, or commanding.

تَبَارَكَ الَّذِي بِيَدِهِ الْمُلْكُ وَهُوَ عَلَىٰ كُلِّ شَيْءٍ قَدِيرٌ ﴿١﴾ الَّذِي **خَلَقَ** الْمَوْتَ وَالْحَيَاةَ

لِيَبْلُوَكُمْ أَيُّكُمْ أَحْسَنُ عَمَلًا ۚ وَهُوَ الْعَزِيزُ الْغَفُورُ ﴿٢﴾ الَّذِي **خَلَقَ** سَبْعَ

سَمَاوَاتٍ طِبَاقًا ۖ مَّا تَرَىٰ فِي خَلْقِ الرَّحْمَٰنِ مِن تَفَاوُتٍ ۖ **فَارْجِعِ** الْبَصَرَ هَلْ تَرَىٰ مِن

فُطُورٍ ﴿٣﴾ ثُمَّ **ارْجِعِ** الْبَصَرَ كَرَّتَيْنِ **يَنقَلِبْ** إِلَيْكَ الْبَصَرُ خَاسِئًا وَهُوَ حَسِيرٌ ﴿٤﴾

وَلَقَدْ **زَيَّنَّا** السَّمَاءَ الدُّنْيَا بِمَصَابِيحَ وَ**جَعَلْنَاهَا** رُجُومًا لِّلشَّيَاطِينِ ۖ وَ**أَعْتَدْنَا** لَهُمْ

عَذَابَ السَّعِيرِ ﴿٥﴾ وَلِلَّذِينَ **كَفَرُوا** بِرَبِّهِمْ عَذَابُ جَهَنَّمَ ۖ وَبِئْسَ الْمَصِيرُ ﴿٦﴾

CHAPTER 6
Review

Date: ______________________

Lesson 1

Accompanying Video
Unit 1: 1.20.1

Learning Goals
- Review all conjugations

A

Watch the accompanying video. Based on what you hear and see in the video, write/circle the correct answer.

1. اِسْتَفْسَرَ is an example of a(n) ______________________ Fi'l.

2. يُنَافِسُ is an example of a(n) ______________________ Fi'l.

3. An inside pronoun is the _________________ that hides inside of the Fi'l.

4. An outside doer can only come with a Fi'l that is in the هُوَ or هِيَ version. It must be after the Fi'l and it must be in _________________ status.

5. Details are extra ______________________ about the Fi'l, all of them are in Nasb status.

6. Questions that answer 'Who?' or 'What?' are مَفْعُوْلٌ بِهِ. Questions that answer 'When?' or '________________?' are مَفْعُوْلٌ فِيْهِ.

7. يَنْصُرُ is in its _________________ form.

8. To turn a Fi'l into forbidding, you have to add لَا and make the Fi'l into its _________________ form.

9. لَنْ means '______________________'.

10. لَمْ means '______________________'.

Date: ____________________

B

Fill in the blanks using the work bank.

How	*Raf'*	*What*	*Nasb*	*After*	*Doer*	*Where*	*Forbidding*
Lightest	*Act*	*Pronoun*	هُوَ	فَاعِلٌ	هِيَ	*Why*	*Present*

1. A Jumlah Fi'liyyah has three parts: the فِعْلٌ, the ______________, and the مَفْعُوْلٌ.

2. The فِعْلٌ is the ______________, the فَاعِلٌ is the ______________, and the مَفْعُوْلٌ is the detail.

3. A doer is always ______________ and a detail is always ______________.

4. The inside pronoun is the ______________ that is inside every فِعْلٌ and the outside doer is an Ism that is Raf' and comes ______________ the فِعْلٌ. Only when an inside doer is ______________ or ______________ can a فِعْلٌ have an outside doer.

5. There are different kinds of details. A مَفْعُوْلٌ بِهِ answers the questions 'Who?' or '______________?'. A مَفْعُوْلٌ فِيْهِ answers 'When?' or '______________?'. A مَفْعُوْلٌ لَهُ answers '______________?'. A مَفْعُوْلٌ حَال answers '______________?'.

6. You learned four kinds of Fi'ls: past tense, ______________ tense, commanding, and ______________.

7. There are three versions of the present tense: normal, light, and ______________.

Date: ____________________

C | Write the conjugations for سَمِعَ, then translate.

سَمِعَ

He heard

Date: ______________________

D | Write the conjugations for يَسْمَعُ, then translate.

يَسْمَعُ

He hears

Date: ____________________

E

Identify each of the following Fi'ls as past tense (P), present tense (PR), commanding (C), or forbidding (F).

1. فَعَلْتُ ____________

2. جَاءَ ____________

3. يَنْصُرُ ____________

4. نُؤْمِنُ ____________

5. اِجْعَلْ ____________

6. سَمِعَا ____________

7. يَرْزُقَ ____________

8. بَشِّرْ ____________

9. جَعَلْتَا ____________

10. أَنْذِرُ ____________

11. اِقْتَرِبْ ____________

12. آمَنُوْا ____________

13. يُنْزِلُ ____________

14. أَسْلَمْتَ ____________

15. أَنْزَلْنَا ____________

16. بَشَّرْتِ ____________

17. لَا تُعَلِّمْ ____________

18. يُنْذِرُوْنَ ____________

19. أَنْذَرْنَ ____________

20. تُفْلِحُوْا ____________

21. لَا تَسْمَعْ ____________

22. جَعَلَا ____________

23. آمَنَتْ ____________

24. بَشَّرُوْا ____________

25. تَنْظُرِيْنَ ____________

26. تُسْلِمْنَ ____________

27. كَتَبَتَا ____________

28. عَلَّمَتْ ____________

29. اُنْظُرْ ____________

30. لَا تُشْرِكُوْا ____________

Date: ____________________

F

Translate the following sentences into English with the help of the definitions given.

	Translation	
To send down: أَنْزَلَ	He sent down the Book	1. أَنْزَلَ الْكِتَابَ
To make: جَعَلَ		2. يَجْعَلُوْنَ الْبَيْتَ
To believe: آمَنَ		3. آمَنَ الرَّسُوْلُ
To warn: أَنْذَرَ		4. حَتَّى يُنْذِرَكُمْ
To hit: ضَرَبَ		5. ضَرَبَ الرَّجُلُ مُوسَى
To help: نَصَرَ		6. نَصَرَ الْمُعَلِّمُ الطَّالِبَ
To succeed: أَفْلَحَ		7. لَنْ تُفْلِحُوْا
To go: ذَهَبَ		8. اِذْهَبْ إِلَى فِرْعَوْنَ
To say: قَالَ		9. قَالَ رَجُلَانِ
To create: خَلَقَ		10. خَلَقَ الْإِنْسَانَ

Date: ____________________

Vocabulary	Translation	
To worship: عَبَدَ	except	11. لَا تَعْبُدُونَ إِلَّا اللَّهَ
To worship: عَبَدَ		12. لَا تَعْبُدُوا الشَّيْطَانَ
To make: جَعَلَ		13. جَعَلْنَاهُ رَجُلًا
To burden: كَلَّفَ		14. لَا يُكَلِّفُ اللَّهُ نَفْسًا
To burden: حَمَّلَ		15. لَا تُحَمِّلْنَا
To enter: دَخَلَ		16. دَخَلْتَ جَنَّتَكَ
To call: دَعَا		17. يَدْعُونَ رَبَّهُمْ
To associate: أَشْرَكَ		18. لَمْ أُشْرِكْ بِرَبِّي
To shun: نَهَرَ		19. لَا تَنْهَرْهُمَا
To return: رَجَعَ		20. ارْجِعِي إِلَى رَبِّكِ
To enter: دَخَلَ		21. ادْخُلِي جَنَّتِي

Date: ______________________

Lesson 2

Accompanying Video
Unit 1: 1.20.2

Learning Goals

- Comprehensive review of the Fi'l through Qur'anic application

A

Watch the accompanying video. Based on what you see in the video, write/circle the correct answer.

1. An Ism has four properties: ______________, number, gender, and type.

2. In عَلَّمَ الْقُرْآنَ, the word اَلْقُرْآنَ is in Nasb status, so it is a(n) ______________.

3. هُوَ is the ______________ pronoun in خَلَقَ الْإِنْسَانَ.

4. In عَلَّمَهُ الْبَيَانَ, the word الْبَيَانَ is a ________________.

   A. مَفْعُوْلٌ بِهِ *B.* مَفْعُوْلٌ فِيْهِ *C.* مَفْعُوْلٌ لَهُ *D.* مَفْعُوْلٌ حَال

5. بِحُسْبَانٍ is a(n) ____________________________ fragment.

6. In اَلنَّجْمُ وَ الشَّجَرُ يَسْجُدَانِ, the doer is ______________.

7. اَلسَّمَاءُ is __________________ in gender.

8. وَضَعَ is a(n) __________________ Fi'l.

Date: ____________________

B

Label each of the highlighted words below as Fi'l, Faa'il, or Maf'ool. If it is a Fi'l, label what tense it is (past, present, command, forbidding). If it is a fragment, label the fragment. If it is a Harf, label what kind of a Harf it is (Jarr/Nasb/light/lightest).

بِسْمِ اللَّهِ الرَّحْمَٰنِ الرَّحِيمِ

الرَّحْمَٰنُ ﴿١﴾ عَلَّمَ الْقُرْآنَ ﴿٢﴾ خَلَقَ الْإِنسَانَ ﴿٣﴾ عَلَّمَهُ الْبَيَانَ ﴿٤﴾ الشَّمْسُ

وَالْقَمَرُ بِحُسْبَانٍ ﴿٥﴾ وَالنَّجْمُ وَالشَّجَرُ يَسْجُدَانِ ﴿٦﴾ وَالسَّمَاءَ رَفَعَهَا وَوَضَعَ

الْمِيزَانَ ﴿٧﴾ أَلَّا تَطْغَوْا فِي الْمِيزَانِ ﴿٨﴾ وَأَقِيمُوا الْوَزْنَ بِالْقِسْطِ وَلَا تُخْسِرُوا

الْمِيزَانَ ﴿٩﴾ وَالْأَرْضَ وَضَعَهَا لِلْأَنَامِ ﴿١٠﴾ فِيهَا فَاكِهَةٌ وَالنَّخْلُ ذَاتُ الْأَكْمَامِ

﴿١١﴾ وَالْحَبُّ ذُو الْعَصْفِ وَالرَّيْحَانُ ﴿١٢﴾ فَبِأَيِّ آلَاءِ رَبِّكُمَا تُكَذِّبَانِ ﴿١٣﴾ خَلَقَ

الْإِنسَانَ مِن صَلْصَالٍ كَالْفَخَّارِ ﴿١٤﴾ وَخَلَقَ الْجَانَّ مِن مَّارِجٍ مِّن نَّارٍ ﴿١٥﴾

Date: ____________________

Words in

Ism

Fi'l

Status

Raf'

Ending sound

- UN: fully flexible
- U: light/partly flexible

Ending combination

- Pair: AANI (heavy) or AA (light)
- Masculine plural: OONA (heavy) or OO (light)
- AATUN (heavy) or AATU (light)

Nasb

Ending sound

- AN: fully flexible
- A: light/partly flexible

Ending combination

- Pair: AYNI (heavy) or AY (light)
- Masculine plural: EENA (heavy) or EE (light)
- AATIN (heavy) or AATI (light)

Jarr

Ending sound

- IN: fully flexible
- I: light

Ending combination

- Pair: AYNI (heavy) or AY (light)
- Masculine plural: EENA (heavy) or EE (light)
- AATIN (heavy) or AATI (light)

Number

Singular

Pair

Normal

- OONA or EENA ending for human masculine plurals
- AATUN or AATIN ending for feminine plurals or non-human plurals

Arabic

Harf

Gender

Plural

Ism Jama'

- قَرْنٌ, نَاسٌ, قَوْمٌ

Broken

- Non-human broken plurals always treated as singular feminine
- Human broken plurals can be treated as sing. feminine or as it is

Masculine

Feminine

Categories

1. Real
2. Fake
   - Ending with ى , ة , آء
   - Broken plurals
   - Feminine because the Arabs said so
   - Body parts in pairs

Type

Common

Proper

Categories

1. Proper names
2. Has ال
3. Pronouns
4. Pointers
5. Ism Mawsool
6. The one being called
7. If the word after 'of' is proper, then the words before 'of' is proper

Frag

Harf + Ism

Harf Jarr

Construction
Harf Jarr + Ism

Rules

- Harf Jarr makes the Ism after it in Jarr status
- Harf of Jarr and its Ism must be next to each other

Harf Jarrs:
ب ت ك ل و مِنْ فِي عَنْ عَلَى حَتَّى إِلَى

Harf Nasb

Construction
Harf Nasb + Ism

Rules

- Harf Nasb makes the Ism in Nasb status
- Harf of Nasb and its Ism do not have to be next to each other

Harf Nasbs:
إِنَّ أَنَّ كَأَنَّ لَيْتَ لَكِنَّ لَعَلَّ بِأَنَّ لِأَنَّ

ments

Ism + Ism

Idhaafah

Construction

Mudhaaf + Mudhaaf Ilayh

Rules

- Mudhaaf = word before ‘of’:
  1. Light,
  2. No ال
- Mudhaaf Ilayh = word after ‘of’:
  1. Always in Jarr status
- Mudhaaf and Mudhaaf Ilayh must be next to each other

Mawsoof Sifah

Construction

Mawsoof + Sifah

Rules

- Mawsoof = noun
- Sifah = adjective
- Mawsoof comes first
- All four properties of Sifah must match all four properties of Mawsoof
- You can have more than one Sifah

Pointers

Construction

Ism Ishaarah + Mushaar Ilayh

Rules

- Ism Ishaarah = pointing word
- Mushaar Ilayh = word being pointed at
- Ism Ishaarah must be followed by ال. If there is no ال it makes a sentence
- All four properties of Ism Ishaarah match all four properties of Mushaar Ilayh
- Ism Ishaarah and Mushaar Ilayh must be next to each other

Words in

Ism

Fi'l

Past

نَصَرَ نَصَرَا نَصَرُوْا

نَصَرَتْ نَصَرَتَا نَصَرْنَ

نَصَرْتَ نَصَرْتُمَا نَصَرْتُمْ

نَصَرْتِ نَصَرْتُمَا نَصَرْتُنَّ

نَصَرْتُ نَصَرْنَا

Present

Normal

يَنْصُرُ يَنْصُرَانِ يَنْصُرُوْنَ

تَنْصُرُ تَنْصُرَانِ يَنْصُرْنَ

تَنْصُرُ تَنْصُرَانِ تَنْصُرُوْنَ

تَنْصُرِيْنَ تَنْصُرَانِ تَنْصُرْنَ

أَنْصُرُ نَنْصُرُ

Light

يَنْصُرَ يَنْصُرَا يَنْصُرُوْا

تَنْصُرَ تَنْصُرَا يَنْصُرْنَ

تَنْصُرَ تَنْصُرَا تَنْصُرُوْا

تَنْصُرِيْ تَنْصُرَا تَنْصُرْنَ

أَنْصُرَ نَنْصُرَ

Arabic

Harf

Commanding

أُنْصُرْ أُنْصُرَا أُنْصُرُوْا

أُنْصُرِيْ أُنْصُرَا أُنْصُرْنَ

Forbidding

لا تَنْصُرْ لا تَنْصُرَا

لا تَنْصُرُوْا

لا تَنْصُرِيْ لا تَنْصُرَا

لا تَنْصُرْنَ

Lightest

يَنْصُرْ يَنْصُرَا يَنْصُرُوْا

تَنْصُرْ تَنْصُرَا يَنْصُرْنَ

تَنْصُرْ تَنْصُرَا تَنْصُرُوْا

تَنْصُرِيْ تَنْصُرَا تَنْصُرْنَ

أَنْصُرْ نَنْصُرْ

MODULE 5
Quranic Application

CHAPTER 1

Surah Kahf

Apply learned grammar concepts to Isms, Fi'ls and Harfs in the first 10 ayahs of the Surah and memorize vocabulary.

CHAPTER 1
Surah Kahf

Date: ____________________

Ayah 1

Accompanying Video
Unit 2: Kahf Ayah 1

Learning Goals

- Apply understanding of grammar to words and fragments
- Memorize vocabulary and translate the ayah

ٱلْحَمْدُ لِلَّهِ ٱلَّذِيٓ أَنزَلَ عَلَىٰ عَبْدِهِ ٱلْكِتَـٰبَ وَلَمْ يَجْعَل لَّهُۥ عِوَجَا ۜ ﴿١﴾

Four properties: ____________________

Translation: ____________________

ٱلْحَمْدُ لِلَّهِ ٱلَّذِيٓ أَنزَلَ عَلَىٰ عَبْدِهِ ٱلْكِتَـٰبَ وَلَمْ يَجْعَل لَّهُۥ عِوَجَا ۜ ﴿١﴾

Fragment: *Idhaafah* *Harf Jarr* *Harf Nasb* *Mawsoof Sifah* *Ism Ishara*
(Circle one)

Fragment breakdown: ____________________ ____________________
(Mudhaaf Ilayh / Victim Sifah / Mushaar Ilayh) (Mudhaaf / Harf Jarr / Harf Nasb Mawsoof / Ism Ishara)

Translation: ____________________

ٱلْحَمْدُ لِلَّهِ ٱلَّذِيٓ أَنزَلَ عَلَىٰ عَبْدِهِ ٱلْكِتَـٰبَ وَلَمْ يَجْعَل لَّهُۥ عِوَجَا ۜ ﴿١﴾

Four properties: ____________________

Translation: ____________________

Date: ____________________

ٱلْحَمْدُ لِلَّهِ ٱلَّذِيٓ أَنزَلَ عَلَىٰ عَبْدِهِ ٱلْكِتَٰبَ وَلَمْ يَجْعَل لَّهُۥ عِوَجَا ۜ ﴿١﴾

Type of Fi'l: (Circle one)

ٱلْمَاضِي	ٱلْمُضَارِع	ٱلْأَمْر	ٱلنَّهْي
Active *Passive*	*Active* *Passive*		
	Normal *Light* *Lightest*		

Inside pronoun: ____________ Translation: ____________

ٱلْحَمْدُ لِلَّهِ ٱلَّذِيٓ أَنزَلَ عَلَىٰ عَبْدِهِ ٱلْكِتَٰبَ وَلَمْ يَجْعَل لَّهُۥ عِوَجَا ۜ ﴿١﴾

First fragment: (Circle one) *Idhaafah* *Harf Jarr* *Harf Nasb* *Mawsoof Sifah* *Ism Ishara*

Fragment breakdown: ____________ (Mudhaaf Ilayh / Victim Sifah / Mushaar Ilayh) ____________ (Mudhaaf / Harf Jarr / Harf Nasb Mawsoof / Ism Ishara)

Second fragment: (Circle one) *Idhaafah* *Harf Jarr* *Harf Nasb* *Mawsoof Sifah* *Ism Ishara*

Fragment breakdown: ____________ (Mudhaaf Ilayh / Victim Sifah / Mushaar Ilayh) ____________ (Mudhaaf / Harf Jarr / Harf Nasb Mawsoof / Ism Ishara)

Translation: ____________

ٱلْحَمْدُ لِلَّهِ ٱلَّذِيٓ أَنزَلَ عَلَىٰ عَبْدِهِ ٱلْكِتَٰبَ وَلَمْ يَجْعَل لَّهُۥ عِوَجَا ۜ ﴿١﴾

Four properties: ____________

Translation: Answer

Date: ____________________

ٱلْحَمْدُ لِلَّهِ ٱلَّذِيٓ أَنزَلَ عَلَىٰ عَبْدِهِ ٱلْكِتَٰبَ وَلَمْ يَجْعَل لَّهُۥ عِوَجَا ۜ ﴿١﴾

Translation: And ____________________

ٱلْحَمْدُ لِلَّهِ ٱلَّذِيٓ أَنزَلَ عَلَىٰ عَبْدِهِ ٱلْكِتَٰبَ وَلَمْ يَجْعَل لَّهُۥ عِوَجَا ۜ ﴿١﴾

Type of Fi'l: ٱلْمَاضِي ٱلْمُضَارِع ٱلْأَمْر ٱلنَّهْي
(Circle one)

Active Passive *Active Passive*

Normal Light Lightest

Inside pronoun: ____________ Translation: ____________

ٱلْحَمْدُ لِلَّهِ ٱلَّذِيٓ أَنزَلَ عَلَىٰ عَبْدِهِ ٱلْكِتَٰبَ وَلَمْ يَجْعَل لَّهُۥ عِوَجَا ۜ ﴿١﴾

Fragment: *Idhaafah Harf Jarr Harf Nasb Mawsoof Sifah Ism Ishara*
(Circle one)

Fragment breakdown: ____________ ____________

(Mudhaaf Ilayh / Victim Sifah / Mushaar Ilayh) (Mudhaaf / Harf Jarr / Harf Nasb Mawsoof / Ism Ishara)

Translation: ____________________

ٱلْحَمْدُ لِلَّهِ ٱلَّذِيٓ أَنزَلَ عَلَىٰ عَبْدِهِ ٱلْكِتَٰبَ وَلَمْ يَجْعَل لَّهُۥ عِوَجَا ۜ ﴿١﴾

Four properties: ____________________

Translation: ____________________

Date: ______________________

ٱلْحَمْدُ لِلَّهِ ٱلَّذِيٓ أَنزَلَ عَلَىٰ عَبْدِهِ ٱلْكِتَٰبَ وَلَمْ يَجْعَل لَّهُۥ عِوَجَا ۜ ﴿١﴾

Translation: ______________________

____

Date: ______________________

Ayah 2

Accompanying Video
Unit 2: Kahf Ayah 2

Learning Goals

- Apply understanding of grammar to words and fragments
- Memorize vocabulary and translate the ayah

قَيِّمًا لِّيُنذِرَ بَأْسًا شَدِيدًا مِّن لَّدُنْهُ

Four properties: ______________________

Translation: ______________________

قَيِّمًا لِّيُنذِرَ بَأْسًا شَدِيدًا مِّن لَّدُنْهُ

Type of Fi'l: الْمَاضِي *Active* *Passive* — الْمُضَارِع *Active* *Passive* / *Normal* *Light* *Lightest* — الْأَمْر — النَّهْي

Inside pronoun: ______________ Translation: ______________________

Date: ______________________

قَيِّمًا لِّيُنذِرَ بَأْسًا شَدِيدًا مِّن لَّدُنْهُ

Fragment: *Idhaafah* *Harf Jarr* *Harf Nasb* *Mawsoof Sifah* *Ism Ishara*

Four properties of بَأْسًا: ______________________

Four properties of شَدِيدًا: ______________________

Fragment breakdown: ______________________ ______________________

Translation: ______________________

قَيِّمًا لِّيُنذِرَ بَأْسًا شَدِيدًا مِّن لَّدُنْهُ

First fragment: *Idhaafah* *Harf Jarr* *Harf Nasb* *Mawsoof Sifah* *Ism Ishara*

Fragment breakdown: ______________________ ______________________

Second fragment: *Idhaafah* *Harf Jarr* *Harf Nasb* *Mawsoof Sifah* *Ism Ishara*

Fragment breakdown: ______________________ ______________________

Translation: ______________________

وَيُبَشِّرَ الْمُؤْمِنِينَ الَّذِينَ يَعْمَلُونَ الصَّالِحَاتِ أَنَّ لَهُمْ أَجْرًا حَسَنًا ﴿٢﴾

Translation: And ______________________

Date: ____________________

وَيُبَشِّرَ الْمُؤْمِنِينَ الَّذِينَ يَعْمَلُونَ الصَّالِحَاتِ أَنَّ لَهُمْ أَجْرًا حَسَنًا ﴿٢﴾

Type of Fi'l: الْمَاضِي *Active Passive* الْمُضَارِع *Active Passive* *Normal Light Lightest* الْأَمْر النَّهي

Inside pronoun: ____________________ Translation: ____________________

Write the past tense chart for the word بَشَّرَ:

______	______	بَشَّرَ
بَشَّرُوا	______	______
______	______	______
______	______	______
	بَشَّرْنَا	______

وَيُبَشِّرَ الْمُؤْمِنِينَ الَّذِينَ يَعْمَلُونَ الصَّالِحَاتِ أَنَّ لَهُمْ أَجْرًا حَسَنًا ﴿٢﴾

Four properties: ____________________

Translation: ____________________

Date: ______________________

وَيُبَشِّرَ الْمُؤْمِنِينَ الَّذِينَ يَعْمَلُونَ الصَّالِحَاتِ أَنَّ لَهُمْ أَجْرًا حَسَنًا ﴿٢﴾

Four properties: Nasb, ______________________

Translation: ______________________

وَيُبَشِّرَ الْمُؤْمِنِينَ الَّذِينَ يَعْمَلُونَ الصَّالِحَاتِ أَنَّ لَهُمْ أَجْرًا حَسَنًا ﴿٢﴾

Type of Fi'l: الْمَاضِي الْمُضَارِع الْأَمْر النَّهي

الْمَاضِي: *Active* *Passive*

الْمُضَارِع: *Active* *Passive*
Normal *Light* *Lightest*

Inside pronoun: ______________ Translation: ______________________

Write the present tense chart for the word يَعْمَلُ:

______	______	يَعْمَلُ
______	______	______
______	______	______
______	______	______
	______	______

Date: ______________________

وَيُبَشِّرَ الْمُؤْمِنِينَ الَّذِينَ يَعْمَلُونَ الصَّالِحَاتِ أَنَّ لَهُمْ أَجْرًا حَسَنًا ﴿٢﴾

Four properties: ______________________

Translation: ______________________

Write the Muslim chart for the word صَالِحَةٌ:

______ ______ ______

______ ______ ______

______ ______ ______

وَيُبَشِّرَ الْمُؤْمِنِينَ الَّذِينَ يَعْمَلُونَ الصَّالِحَاتِ أَنَّ لَهُمْ أَجْرًا حَسَنًا ﴿٢﴾

Fragment: *Idhaafah* *Harf Jarr* *Harf Nasb* *Mawsoof Sifah* *Ism Ishara*

Fragment breakdown: ______________ ______________

Translation: ______________________

Date: ____________________

وَيُبَشِّرَ الْمُؤْمِنِينَ الَّذِينَ يَعْمَلُونَ الصَّالِحَاتِ أَنَّ لَهُمْ أَجْرًا حَسَنًا ﴿٢﴾

First fragment: *Idhaafah* *Harf Jarr* *Harf Nasb* *Mawsoof Sifah* *Ism Ishara*

Fragment breakdown: ____________________ ____________________

Second fragment: *Idhaafah* *Harf Jarr* *Harf Nasb* *Mawsoof Sifah* *Ism Ishara*

Four properties of أَجْرًا: ____________________

Four properties of حَسَنًا: ____________________

Fragment breakdown: ____________________ ____________________

Translation: ____________________

قَيِّمًا لِّيُنذِرَ بَأْسًا شَدِيدًا مِّن لَّدُنْهُ وَيُبَشِّرَ الْمُؤْمِنِينَ الَّذِينَ يَعْمَلُونَ الصَّالِحَاتِ أَنَّ لَهُمْ أَجْرًا حَسَنًا ﴿٢﴾

Translation: ____________________

____

Date: ______________________

Ayah 3-4

Accompanying Video
Unit 2: Kahf Ayah 3-5

Learning Goals

- Apply understanding of grammar to words and fragments
- Memorize vocabulary and translate the ayah

مَّا كِثِينَ فِيهِ أَبَدًا ﴿٣﴾ وَيُنذِرَ الَّذِينَ قَالُوا اتَّخَذَ اللَّهُ وَلَدًا ﴿٤﴾

Four properties: ______________________

Translation: ______________________

مَّا كِثِينَ فِيهِ أَبَدًا ﴿٣﴾ وَيُنذِرَ الَّذِينَ قَالُوا اتَّخَذَ اللَّهُ وَلَدًا ﴿٤﴾

Fragment: *Idhaafah* *Harf Jarr* *Harf Nasb* *Mawsoof Sifah* *Ism Ishara*

Fragment breakdown: ______________________ ______________________

Translation: ______________________

مَّا كِثِينَ فِيهِ أَبَدًا ﴿٣﴾ وَيُنذِرَ الَّذِينَ قَالُوا اتَّخَذَ اللَّهُ وَلَدًا ﴿٤﴾

Four properties: ______________________

Translation: ______________________

Date: ______________________

مَّا كِثِينَ فِيهِ أَبَدًا ۝٣ وَيُنذِرَ الَّذِينَ قَالُوا اتَّخَذَ اللَّهُ وَلَدًا ۝٤

Translation: ______________________

مَّا كِثِينَ فِيهِ أَبَدًا ۝٣ وَيُنذِرَ الَّذِينَ قَالُوا اتَّخَذَ اللَّهُ وَلَدًا ۝٤

Type of Fi'l: الْمَاضِي — *Active* *Passive*

الْمُضَارِع — *Active* *Passive*

Normal *Light* *Lightest*

الْأَمْر

النَّهي

Inside pronoun: ______________________ Translation: ______________________

مَّا كِثِينَ فِيهِ أَبَدًا ۝٣ وَيُنذِرَ الَّذِينَ قَالُوا اتَّخَذَ اللَّهُ وَلَدًا ۝٤

Four properties: ______________________

Translation: ______________________

Write the Ism Mawsool chart:

______	______	______
______	______	______

Date: ______________________

مَّاكِثِينَ فِيهِ أَبَدًا ﴿٣﴾ وَيُنذِرَ الَّذِينَ قَالُوا اتَّخَذَ اللَّهُ وَلَدًا ﴿٤﴾

Type of Fi'l: الْمَاضِي الْمُضَارِع الْأَمْر النَّهي

Active *Passive* *Active* *Passive*

Normal *Light* *Lightest*

Inside pronoun: ______________ Translation: ______________

مَّاكِثِينَ فِيهِ أَبَدًا ﴿٣﴾ وَيُنذِرَ الَّذِينَ قَالُوا اتَّخَذَ اللَّهُ وَلَدًا ﴿٤﴾

Type of Fi'l: الْمَاضِي الْمُضَارِع الْأَمْر النَّهي

Active *Passive* *Active* *Passive*

Normal *Light* *Lightest*

Inside pronoun: ______________ Translation: ______________

مَّاكِثِينَ فِيهِ أَبَدًا ﴿٣﴾ وَيُنذِرَ الَّذِينَ قَالُوا اتَّخَذَ اللَّهُ وَلَدًا ﴿٤﴾

Four properties: ______________

Translation: ______________

مَّاكِثِينَ فِيهِ أَبَدًا ﴿٣﴾ وَيُنذِرَ الَّذِينَ قَالُوا اتَّخَذَ اللَّهُ وَلَدًا ﴿٤﴾

Four properties: ______________

Translation: ______________

Date: ______________________

مَّاكِثِينَ فِيهِ أَبَدًا ﴿٣﴾ وَيُنذِرَ الَّذِينَ قَالُوا اتَّخَذَ اللَّهُ وَلَدًا ﴿٤﴾

Translation: ____

____

Date: ______________________________

Ayah 5

Accompanying Video
Unit 2: Kahf Ayah 3-5

Learning Goals

- Apply understanding of grammar to words and fragments
- Memorize vocabulary and translate the ayah

مَّا لَهُم بِهِۦ مِنْ عِلْمٍ وَلَا لِءَابَآئِهِمْ ۚ كَبُرَتْ كَلِمَةً تَخْرُجُ مِنْ أَفْوَٰهِهِمْ ۚ إِن يَقُولُونَ إِلَّا كَذِبًا ﴿٥﴾

Translation: Not ______________________________

مَّا لَهُم بِهِۦ مِنْ عِلْمٍ وَلَا لِءَابَآئِهِمْ ۚ كَبُرَتْ كَلِمَةً تَخْرُجُ مِنْ أَفْوَٰهِهِمْ ۚ إِن يَقُولُونَ إِلَّا كَذِبًا ﴿٥﴾

Fragment: *Idhaafah* *Harf Jarr* *Harf Nasb* *Mawsoof Sifah* *Ism Ishara*

Fragment breakdown: ______________________ ______________________

Translation: ______________________________

مَّا لَهُم بِهِۦ مِنْ عِلْمٍ وَلَا لِءَابَآئِهِمْ ۚ كَبُرَتْ كَلِمَةً تَخْرُجُ مِنْ أَفْوَٰهِهِمْ ۚ إِن يَقُولُونَ إِلَّا كَذِبًا ﴿٥﴾

Fragment: *Idhaafah* *Harf Jarr* *Harf Nasb* *Mawsoof Sifah* *Ism Ishara*

Fragment breakdown: ______________________ ______________________

Translation: ______________________________

Date: ____________________

مَّا لَهُم بِهِۦ مِنْ عِلْمٍ وَلَا لِءَابَآئِهِمْ ۚ كَبُرَتْ كَلِمَةً تَخْرُجُ مِنْ أَفْوَٰهِهِمْ ۚ إِن يَقُولُونَ إِلَّا كَذِبًا ٥

Fragment: *Idhaafah* *Harf Jarr* *Harf Nasb* *Mawsoof Sifah* *Ism Ishara*

Fragment breakdown: ____________________ ____________________

Translation: ____________________

مَّا لَهُم بِهِۦ مِنْ عِلْمٍ وَلَا لِءَابَآئِهِمْ ۚ كَبُرَتْ كَلِمَةً تَخْرُجُ مِنْ أَفْوَٰهِهِمْ ۚ إِن يَقُولُونَ إِلَّا كَذِبًا ٥

Translation: ____________________

مَّا لَهُم بِهِۦ مِنْ عِلْمٍ وَلَا لِءَابَآئِهِمْ ۚ كَبُرَتْ كَلِمَةً تَخْرُجُ مِنْ أَفْوَٰهِهِمْ ۚ إِن يَقُولُونَ إِلَّا كَذِبًا ٥

Translation: ____________________

مَّا لَهُم بِهِۦ مِنْ عِلْمٍ وَلَا لِءَابَآئِهِمْ ۚ كَبُرَتْ كَلِمَةً تَخْرُجُ مِنْ أَفْوَٰهِهِمْ ۚ إِن يَقُولُونَ إِلَّا كَذِبًا ٥

First fragment: *Idhaafah* *Harf Jarr* *Harf Nasb* *Mawsoof Sifah* *Ism Ishara*

Fragment breakdown: ____________________ ____________________

Second fragment: *Idhaafah* *Harf Jarr* *Harf Nasb* *Mawsoof Sifah* *Ism Ishara*

Fragment breakdown: ____________________ ____________________

Translation: ____________________

Date: ____________________

مَّا لَهُم بِهِۦ مِنْ عِلْمٍ وَلَا لِآبَآئِهِمْ ۚ كَبُرَتْ كَلِمَةً تَخْرُجُ مِنْ أَفْوَاهِهِمْ ۚ إِن يَقُولُونَ إِلَّا كَذِبًا ﴿٥﴾

Type of Fi'l: الْمَاضِي — *Active* *Passive* | الْمُضَارِع — *Active* *Passive*; *Normal* *Light* *Lightest* | الْأَمْر | النَّهي

Inside pronoun: ____________ Translation: ____________________

مَّا لَهُم بِهِۦ مِنْ عِلْمٍ وَلَا لِآبَآئِهِمْ ۚ كَبُرَتْ كَلِمَةً تَخْرُجُ مِنْ أَفْوَاهِهِمْ ۚ إِن يَقُولُونَ إِلَّا كَذِبًا ﴿٥﴾

Four properties: ____________________

Translation: ____________________

مَّا لَهُم بِهِۦ مِنْ عِلْمٍ وَلَا لِآبَآئِهِمْ ۚ كَبُرَتْ كَلِمَةً تَخْرُجُ مِنْ أَفْوَاهِهِمْ ۚ إِن يَقُولُونَ إِلَّا كَذِبًا ﴿٥﴾

Type of Fi'l: الْمَاضِي — *Active* *Passive* | الْمُضَارِع — *Active* *Passive*; *Normal* *Light* *Lightest* | الْأَمْر | النَّهي

Inside pronoun: ____________ Translation: ____________________

Date: _____

مَّا لَهُم بِهِۦ مِنۡ عِلۡمٖ وَلَا لِأٓبَآئِهِمۡۚ كَبُرَتۡ كَلِمَةٗ تَخۡرُجُ مِنۡ أَفۡوَٰهِهِمۡۚ إِن يَقُولُونَ إِلَّا كَذِبٗا ۝

First fragment: *Idhaafah   Harf Jarr   Harf Nasb   Mawsoof Sifah   Ism Ishara*

Fragment breakdown: _____   _____

Second fragment: *Idhaafah   Harf Jarr   Harf Nasb   Mawsoof Sifah   Ism Ishara*

Fragment breakdown: _____   _____

Translation: _____

مَّا لَهُم بِهِۦ مِنۡ عِلۡمٖ وَلَا لِأٓبَآئِهِمۡۚ كَبُرَتۡ كَلِمَةٗ تَخۡرُجُ مِنۡ أَفۡوَاهِهِمۡۚ إِن يَقُولُونَ إِلَّا كَذِبٗا ۝

Translation: Not _____

مَّا لَهُم بِهِۦ مِنۡ عِلۡمٖ وَلَا لِأٓبَآئِهِمۡۚ كَبُرَتۡ كَلِمَةٗ تَخۡرُجُ مِنۡ أَفۡوَاهِهِمۡۚ إِن يَقُولُونَ إِلَّا كَذِبٗا ۝

Type of Fi'l: الْمَاضِي   الْمُضَارِع   الْأَمْر   النَّهْي
                  Active Passive   Active Passive
                                       Normal Light Lightest

Inside pronoun: _____   Translation: _____

Date: ____________________

Write the present tense chart for the word يَقُوْلُ:

______	______	يَقُوْلُ
يَقُلْنَ	______	______
______	______	______
______	______	______
	نَقُوْلُ	______

مَّا لَهُم بِهِۦ مِنْ عِلْمٍ وَلَا لِآبَآئِهِمْ ۚ كَبُرَتْ كَلِمَةً تَخْرُجُ مِنْ أَفْوَٰهِهِمْ ۚ إِن يَقُولُونَ إِلَّا كَذِبًا ﴿٥﴾

Translation: ____________________

مَّا لَهُم بِهِۦ مِنْ عِلْمٍ وَلَا لِآبَآئِهِمْ ۚ كَبُرَتْ كَلِمَةً تَخْرُجُ مِنْ أَفْوَٰهِهِمْ ۚ إِن يَقُولُونَ إِلَّا كَذِبًا ﴿٥﴾

Four properties: ____________________

Translation: ____________________

Date: ______________________

مَّا لَهُم بِهِۦ مِنْ عِلْمٍ وَلَا لِءَابَآئِهِمْ ۚ كَبُرَتْ كَلِمَةً تَخْرُجُ مِنْ أَفْوَٰهِهِمْ ۚ إِن يَقُولُونَ إِلَّا كَذِبًا ﴿٥﴾

Translation: ____

____

Date: ____________________

Ayah 6

Accompanying Video
Unit 2: Kahf Ayah 6

Learning Goals

- Apply understanding of grammar to words and fragments
- Memorize vocabulary and translate the ayah

فَلَعَلَّكَ بَاخِعٌ نَّفْسَكَ عَلَىٰٓ ءَاثَٰرِهِمْ إِن لَّمْ يُؤْمِنُوا۟ بِهَٰذَا ٱلْحَدِيثِ أَسَفًا ﴿٦﴾

Translation: So ____________________

فَلَعَلَّكَ بَاخِعٌ نَّفْسَكَ عَلَىٰٓ ءَاثَٰرِهِمْ إِن لَّمْ يُؤْمِنُوا۟ بِهَٰذَا ٱلْحَدِيثِ أَسَفًا ﴿٦﴾

Fragment: *Idhaafah* *Harf Jarr* *Harf Nasb* *Mawsoof Sifah* *Ism Ishara*

Fragment breakdown: ____________________ ____________________

Translation: ____________________

فَلَعَلَّكَ بَاخِعٌ نَّفْسَكَ عَلَىٰٓ ءَاثَٰرِهِمْ إِن لَّمْ يُؤْمِنُوا۟ بِهَٰذَا ٱلْحَدِيثِ أَسَفًا ﴿٦﴾

Four properties: ____________________

Translation: ____________________

Date: ____________________

فَلَعَلَّكَ بَاخِعٌ نَّفْسَكَ عَلَىٰٓ ءَاثَـٰرِهِمْ إِن لَّمْ يُؤْمِنُوا۟ بِهَـٰذَا ٱلْحَدِيثِ أَسَفًا ﴿٦﴾

Fragment: *Idhaafah* *Harf Jarr* *Harf Nasb* *Mawsoof Sifah* *Ism Ishara*

Fragment breakdown: ____________________ ____________________

Translation: ____________________

فَلَعَلَّكَ بَاخِعٌ نَّفْسَكَ عَلَىٰٓ ءَاثَـٰرِهِمْ إِن لَّمْ يُؤْمِنُوا۟ بِهَـٰذَا ٱلْحَدِيثِ أَسَفًا ﴿٦﴾

First fragment: *Idhaafah* *Harf Jarr* *Harf Nasb* *Mawsoof Sifah* *Ism Ishara*

Fragment breakdown: ____________________ ____________________

Second fragment: *Idhaafah* *Harf Jarr* *Harf Nasb* *Mawsoof Sifah* *Ism Ishara*

Fragment breakdown: ____________________ ____________________

Translation: ____________________

فَلَعَلَّكَ بَاخِعٌ نَّفْسَكَ عَلَىٰٓ ءَاثَـٰرِهِمْ إِن لَّمْ يُؤْمِنُوا۟ بِهَـٰذَا ٱلْحَدِيثِ أَسَفًا ﴿٦﴾

Translation: ____________________

Date: ______________________

فَلَعَلَّكَ بَاخِعٌ نَّفْسَكَ عَلَىٰٓ آثَارِهِمْ إِن لَّمْ يُؤْمِنُوا بِهَٰذَا الْحَدِيثِ أَسَفًا ﴿٦﴾

Type of Fi'l: الْمَاضِي الْمُضَارِع الْأَمْر النَّهْي

Active *Passive*

Active *Passive*

Normal *Light* *Lightest*

Inside pronoun: ______________ Translation: ______________________

فَلَعَلَّكَ بَاخِعٌ نَّفْسَكَ عَلَىٰٓ آثَارِهِمْ إِن لَّمْ يُؤْمِنُوا بِهَٰذَا الْحَدِيثِ أَسَفًا ﴿٦﴾

First fragment: *Idhaafah* *Harf Jarr* *Harf Nasb* *Mawsoof Sifah* *Ism Ishara*

Fragment breakdown: ______________________ ______________________

Second fragment: *Idhaafah* *Harf Jarr* *Harf Nasb* *Mawsoof Sifah* *Ism Ishara*

Fragment breakdown: ______________________ ______________________

Translation: ______________________________

فَلَعَلَّكَ بَاخِعٌ نَّفْسَكَ عَلَىٰٓ آثَارِهِمْ إِن لَّمْ يُؤْمِنُوا بِهَٰذَا الْحَدِيثِ أَسَفًا ﴿٦﴾

Four properties: ______________________________

Translation: ______________________________

Date: ____________________

فَلَعَلَّكَ بَاخِعٌ نَّفْسَكَ عَلَىٰٓ ءَاثَٰرِهِمْ إِن لَّمْ يُؤْمِنُوا۟ بِهَٰذَا ٱلْحَدِيثِ أَسَفًا ٦

Translation: ____________________

____

Date: ____________________

Ayah 7

Accompanying Video
Unit 2: Kahf Ayah 7

Learning Goals

- Apply understanding of grammar to words and fragments
- Memorize vocabulary and translate the ayah

إِنَّا جَعَلْنَا مَا عَلَى الْأَرْضِ زِينَةً لَّهَا لِنَبْلُوَهُمْ أَيُّهُمْ أَحْسَنُ عَمَلًا ﴿٧﴾

Fragment: *Idhaafah* *Harf Jarr* *Harf Nasb* *Mawsoof Sifah* *Ism Ishara*

Fragment breakdown: ____________________ ____________________

Translation: ____________________

إِنَّا جَعَلْنَا مَا عَلَى الْأَرْضِ زِينَةً لَّهَا لِنَبْلُوَهُمْ أَيُّهُمْ أَحْسَنُ عَمَلًا ﴿٧﴾

Type of Fi'l: الْمَاضِي (*Active* *Passive*) الْمُضَارِع (*Active* *Passive*; *Normal* *Light* *Lightest*) الْأَمْر النَّهْي

Inside pronoun: ____________________ Translation: ____________________

إِنَّا جَعَلْنَا مَا عَلَى الْأَرْضِ زِينَةً لَّهَا لِنَبْلُوَهُمْ أَيُّهُمْ أَحْسَنُ عَمَلًا ﴿٧﴾

Translation: ____________________

Date: ____________________

إِنَّا جَعَلْنَا مَا عَلَى ٱلْأَرْضِ زِينَةً لَّهَا لِنَبْلُوَهُمْ أَيُّهُمْ أَحْسَنُ عَمَلًا ﴿٧﴾

Fragment: *Idhaafah* *Harf Jarr* *Harf Nasb* *Mawsoof Sifah* *Ism Ishara*

Fragment breakdown: ____________________ ____________________

Translation: ____________________

إِنَّا جَعَلْنَا مَا عَلَى ٱلْأَرْضِ زِينَةً لَّهَا لِنَبْلُوَهُمْ أَيُّهُمْ أَحْسَنُ عَمَلًا ﴿٧﴾

Four properties: ____________________

Translation: ____________________

إِنَّا جَعَلْنَا مَا عَلَى ٱلْأَرْضِ زِينَةً لَّهَا لِنَبْلُوَهُمْ أَيُّهُمْ أَحْسَنُ عَمَلًا ﴿٧﴾

Fragment: *Idhaafah* *Harf Jarr* *Harf Nasb* *Mawsoof Sifah* *Ism Ishara*

Fragment breakdown: ____________________ ____________________

Translation: ____________________

Date: ____________________

إِنَّا جَعَلْنَا مَا عَلَى الْأَرْضِ زِينَةً لَّهَا لِنَبْلُوَهُمْ أَيُّهُمْ أَحْسَنُ عَمَلًا ﴿٧﴾

Type of Fi'l: الْمَاضِي الْمُضَارِع الْأَمْر النَّهْي

Active *Passive* *Active* *Passive*

Normal *Light* *Lightest*

Inside pronoun: ____________________ Translation: ____________________

إِنَّا جَعَلْنَا مَا عَلَى الْأَرْضِ زِينَةً لَّهَا لِنَبْلُوَهُمْ أَيُّهُمْ أَحْسَنُ عَمَلًا ﴿٧﴾

Fragment: *Idhaafah* *Harf Jarr* *Harf Nasb* *Mawsoof Sifah* *Ism Ishara*

Fragment breakdown: ____________________ ____________________

Translation: ____________________

إِنَّا جَعَلْنَا مَا عَلَى الْأَرْضِ زِينَةً لَّهَا لِنَبْلُوَهُمْ أَيُّهُمْ أَحْسَنُ عَمَلًا ﴿٧﴾

Four properties: ____________________

Translation: ____________________

إِنَّا جَعَلْنَا مَا عَلَى الْأَرْضِ زِينَةً لَّهَا لِنَبْلُوَهُمْ أَيُّهُمْ أَحْسَنُ عَمَلًا ﴿٧﴾

Four properties: ____________________

Translation: ____________________

Date: ______________________

إِنَّا جَعَلْنَا مَا عَلَى ٱلْأَرْضِ زِينَةً لَّهَا لِنَبْلُوَهُمْ أَيُّهُمْ أَحْسَنُ عَمَلًا ﴿٧﴾

Translation: ____

____

Date: ____________

Ayah 8

Accompanying Video
Unit 2: Kahf Ayah 8

Learning Goals

- Apply understanding of grammar to words and fragments
- Memorize vocabulary and translate the ayah

وَإِنَّا لَجَاعِلُونَ مَا عَلَيْهَا صَعِيدًا جُرُزًا ﴿٨﴾

Translation: ____________

وَإِنَّا لَجَاعِلُونَ مَا عَلَيْهَا صَعِيدًا جُرُزًا ﴿٨﴾

Fragment: *Idhaafah* *Harf Jarr* *Harf Nasb* *Mawsoof Sifah* *Ism Ishara*

Fragment breakdown: ____________ ____________

Translation: ____________

وَإِنَّا لَجَاعِلُونَ مَا عَلَيْهَا صَعِيدًا جُرُزًا ﴿٨﴾

Translation: No doubt

وَإِنَّا لَجَاعِلُونَ مَا عَلَيْهَا صَعِيدًا جُرُزًا ﴿٨﴾

Four properties: ____________

Translation: ____________

Date: ______________________

Write the Muslim chart for the word جَاعِلٌ:

______________ ______________ ______________

______________ ______________ ______________

______________ ______________ ______________

وَإِنَّا لَجَاعِلُونَ مَا عَلَيْهَا صَعِيدًا جُرُزًا ﴿٨﴾

Translation: What ______________________

وَإِنَّا لَجَاعِلُونَ مَا عَلَيْهَا صَعِيدًا جُرُزًا ﴿٨﴾

Fragment: *Idhaafah* *Harf Jarr* *Harf Nasb* *Mawsoof Sifah* *Ism Ishara*

Fragment breakdown: ______________________ ______________________

Translation: ______________________

Date: ______________________

وَإِنَّا لَجَٰعِلُونَ مَا عَلَيْهَا صَعِيدًا جُرُزًا ﴿٨﴾

Fragment: *Idhaafah* *Harf Jarr* *Harf Nasb* *Mawsoof Sifah* *Ism Ishara*

Four properties of صَعِيدًا: ______________________

Four properties of جُرُزًا: ______________________

Fragment breakdown: ______________________ ______________________

Translation: ______________________

وَإِنَّا لَجَٰعِلُونَ مَا عَلَيْهَا صَعِيدًا جُرُزًا ﴿٨﴾

Translation: ______________________

Date: ____________________

Ayah 9

Accompanying Video
Unit 2: Kahf Ayah 9

Learning Goals

- Apply understanding of grammar to words and fragments
- Memorize vocabulary and translate the ayah

أَمْ حَسِبْتَ أَنَّ أَصْحَابَ الْكَهْفِ وَالرَّقِيمِ كَانُوا مِنْ آيَاتِنَا عَجَبًا ﴿٩﴾

Translation: Or ____________________

أَمْ حَسِبْتَ أَنَّ أَصْحَابَ الْكَهْفِ وَالرَّقِيمِ كَانُوا مِنْ آيَاتِنَا عَجَبًا ﴿٩﴾

Type of Fi'l: الْمَاضِي *Active* *Passive* | الْمُضَارِع *Active* *Passive* / *Normal* *Light* *Lightest* | الْأَمْر | النَّهي

Inside pronoun: ____________________ Translation: ____________________

أَمْ حَسِبْتَ أَنَّ أَصْحَابَ الْكَهْفِ وَالرَّقِيمِ كَانُوا مِنْ آيَاتِنَا عَجَبًا ﴿٩﴾

Fragment: *Idhaafah* *Harf Jarr* *Harf Nasb* *Mawsoof Sifah* *Ism Ishara*

Fragment breakdown: ____________________ ____________________

Translation: ____________________

Date: ____________

أَمْ حَسِبْتَ أَنَّ أَصْحَابَ الْكَهْفِ وَالرَّقِيمِ كَانُوا مِنْ آيَاتِنَا عَجَبًا ﴿٩﴾

Fragment: *Idhaafah* *Harf Jarr* *Harf Nasb* *Mawsoof Sifah* *Ism Ishara*

Fragment breakdown: ____________ ____________

Translation: ____________

أَمْ حَسِبْتَ أَنَّ أَصْحَابَ الْكَهْفِ وَالرَّقِيمِ كَانُوا مِنْ آيَاتِنَا عَجَبًا ﴿٩﴾

First fragment: *Idhaafah* *Harf Jarr* *Harf Nasb* *Mawsoof Sifah* *Ism Ishara*

Four properties of أَصْحَابَ: ____________

Fragment breakdown: ____________ ____________

Second fragment: *Idhaafah* *Harf Jarr* *Harf Nasb* *Mawsoof Sifah* *Ism Ishara*

Four properties of الْكَهْفِ: ____________

Four properties of الرَّقِيم: ____________

Fragment breakdown: ____________ ____________

Translation: ____________

Date: ____________________

أَمْ حَسِبْتَ أَنَّ أَصْحَابَ الْكَهْفِ وَالرَّقِيمِ كَانُوا مِنْ آيَاتِنَا عَجَبًا ﴿٩﴾

Type of Fi'l: الْمَاضِي *Active* *Passive* الْمُضَارِع *Active* *Passive* *Normal* *Light* *Lightest* الْأَمْر النَّهي

Inside pronoun: ____________________ Translation: ____________________

أَمْ حَسِبْتَ أَنَّ أَصْحَابَ الْكَهْفِ وَالرَّقِيمِ كَانُوا مِنْ آيَاتِنَا عَجَبًا ﴿٩﴾

First fragment: *Idhaafah* *Harf Jarr* *Harf Nasb* *Mawsoof Sifah* *Ism Ishara*

Fragment breakdown: ____________________ ____________________

Second fragment: *Idhaafah* *Harf Jarr* *Harf Nasb* *Mawsoof Sifah* *Ism Ishara*

Fragment breakdown: ____________________ ____________________

Translation: ____________________

أَمْ حَسِبْتَ أَنَّ أَصْحَابَ الْكَهْفِ وَالرَّقِيمِ كَانُوا مِنْ آيَاتِنَا عَجَبًا ﴿٩﴾

Four properties: ____________________

Translation: ____________________

Date: ____________________

أَمْ حَسِبْتَ أَنَّ أَصْحَابَ الْكَهْفِ وَالرَّقِيمِ كَانُوا مِنْ آيَاتِنَا عَجَبًا ﴿٩﴾

Translation: ____________________

____

Date: ______________________

Ayah 10

Accompanying Video
Unit 2: Kahf Ayah 10

Learning Goals

- Apply understanding of grammar to words and fragments
- Memorize vocabulary and translate the ayah

إِذْ أَوَى الْفِتْيَةُ إِلَى الْكَهْفِ فَقَالُوا رَبَّنَا آتِنَا مِن لَّدُنكَ رَحْمَةً وَهَيِّئْ لَنَا مِنْ أَمْرِنَا رَشَدًا ﴿١٠﴾

Translation: Remember when ______________________

إِذْ أَوَى الْفِتْيَةُ إِلَى الْكَهْفِ فَقَالُوا رَبَّنَا آتِنَا مِن لَّدُنكَ رَحْمَةً وَهَيِّئْ لَنَا مِنْ أَمْرِنَا رَشَدًا ﴿١٠﴾

Type of Fi'l: الْمَاضِي — *Active* *Passive* | الْمُضَارِع — *Active* *Passive* / *Normal* *Light* *Lightest* | الْأَمْر | النَّهي

Inside pronoun: ______________ Translation: ______________________

إِذْ أَوَى الْفِتْيَةُ إِلَى الْكَهْفِ فَقَالُوا رَبَّنَا آتِنَا مِن لَّدُنكَ رَحْمَةً وَهَيِّئْ لَنَا مِنْ أَمْرِنَا رَشَدًا ﴿١٠﴾

Four properties: ______________________

Translation: ______________________

Date: ____________________

إِذْ أَوَى الْفِتْيَةُ إِلَى الْكَهْفِ فَقَالُوا رَبَّنَا آتِنَا مِن لَّدُنكَ رَحْمَةً وَهَيِّئْ لَنَا مِنْ أَمْرِنَا رَشَدًا ﴿١٠﴾

Fragment: *Idhaafah* *Harf Jarr* *Harf Nasb* *Mawsoof Sifah* *Ism Ishara*

Fragment breakdown: ____________________ ____________________

Translation: ____________________

إِذْ أَوَى الْفِتْيَةُ إِلَى الْكَهْفِ فَقَالُوا رَبَّنَا آتِنَا مِن لَّدُنكَ رَحْمَةً وَهَيِّئْ لَنَا مِنْ أَمْرِنَا رَشَدًا ﴿١٠﴾

Translation: ____________________

إِذْ أَوَى الْفِتْيَةُ إِلَى الْكَهْفِ فَقَالُوا رَبَّنَا آتِنَا مِن لَّدُنكَ رَحْمَةً وَهَيِّئْ لَنَا مِنْ أَمْرِنَا رَشَدًا ﴿١٠﴾

Type of Fi'l: الْمَاضِي الْمُضَارِع الْأَمْر النَّهي

Active *Passive* (الْمَاضِي)

Active *Passive* (الْمُضَارِع)

Normal *Light* *Lightest*

Inside pronoun: ____________________ Translation: ____________________

إِذْ أَوَى الْفِتْيَةُ إِلَى الْكَهْفِ فَقَالُوا رَبَّنَا آتِنَا مِن لَّدُنكَ رَحْمَةً وَهَيِّئْ لَنَا مِنْ أَمْرِنَا رَشَدًا ﴿١٠﴾

Fragment: *Idhaafah* *Harf Jarr* *Harf Nasb* *Mawsoof Sifah* *Ism Ishara*

Fragment breakdown: ____________________ ____________________

Translation: ____________________

Date: __________

إِذْ أَوَى الْفِتْيَةُ إِلَى الْكَهْفِ فَقَالُوا رَبَّنَا آتِنَا مِن لَّدُنكَ رَحْمَةً وَهَيِّئْ لَنَا مِنْ أَمْرِنَا رَشَدًا ﴿١٠﴾

Type of Fi'l: الْمَاضِي *Active* *Passive* الْمُضَارِع *Active* *Passive* *Normal* *Light* *Lightest* الْأَمْر النَّهي

Inside pronoun: __________ Translation: __________

إِذْ أَوَى الْفِتْيَةُ إِلَى الْكَهْفِ فَقَالُوا رَبَّنَا آتِنَا مِن لَّدُنكَ رَحْمَةً وَهَيِّئْ لَنَا مِنْ أَمْرِنَا رَشَدًا ﴿١٠﴾

First fragment: *Idhaafah* *Harf Jarr* *Harf Nasb* *Mawsoof Sifah* *Ism Ishara*

Fragment breakdown: __________ __________

Second fragment: *Idhaafah* *Harf Jarr* *Harf Nasb* *Mawsoof Sifah* *Ism Ishara*

Fragment breakdown: __________ __________

Translation: Answer

إِذْ أَوَى الْفِتْيَةُ إِلَى الْكَهْفِ فَقَالُوا رَبَّنَا آتِنَا مِن لَّدُنكَ رَحْمَةً وَهَيِّئْ لَنَا مِنْ أَمْرِنَا رَشَدًا ﴿١٠﴾

Four properties: __________

Translation: __________

Date: ______

إِذْ أَوَى الْفِتْيَةُ إِلَى الْكَهْفِ فَقَالُوا رَبَّنَا آتِنَا مِن لَّدُنكَ رَحْمَةً وَهَيِّئْ لَنَا مِنْ أَمْرِنَا رَشَدًا ﴿١٠﴾

Translation: ______

إِذْ أَوَى الْفِتْيَةُ إِلَى الْكَهْفِ فَقَالُوا رَبَّنَا آتِنَا مِن لَّدُنكَ رَحْمَةً وَهَيِّئْ لَنَا مِنْ أَمْرِنَا رَشَدًا ﴿١٠﴾

Type of Fi'l: الْمَاضِي — *Active* *Passive*; الْمُضَارِع — *Active* *Passive*, *Normal* *Light* *Lightest*; الْأَمْر; النَّهي

Inside pronoun: ______ Translation: ______

إِذْ أَوَى الْفِتْيَةُ إِلَى الْكَهْفِ فَقَالُوا رَبَّنَا آتِنَا مِن لَّدُنكَ رَحْمَةً وَهَيِّئْ لَنَا مِنْ أَمْرِنَا رَشَدًا ﴿١٠﴾

Fragment: *Idhaafah* *Harf Jarr* *Harf Nasb* *Mawsoof Sifah* *Ism Ishara*

Fragment breakdown: ______ ______

Translation: ______

Date: ____________________

إِذۡ أَوَى ٱلۡفِتۡيَةُ إِلَى ٱلۡكَهۡفِ فَقَالُواْ رَبَّنَآ ءَاتِنَا مِن لَّدُنكَ رَحۡمَةٗ وَهَيِّئۡ لَنَا **مِنۡ أَمۡرِنَا** رَشَدٗا ١٠

First fragment: *Idhaafah* *Harf Jarr* *Harf Nasb* *Mawsoof Sifah* *Ism Ishara*

Fragment breakdown: ____________________ ____________________

Second fragment: *Idhaafah* *Harf Jarr* *Harf Nasb* *Mawsoof Sifah* *Ism Ishara*

Fragment breakdown: ____________________ ____________________

Translation: ____________________

إِذۡ أَوَى ٱلۡفِتۡيَةُ إِلَى ٱلۡكَهۡفِ فَقَالُواْ رَبَّنَآ ءَاتِنَا مِن لَّدُنكَ رَحۡمَةٗ وَهَيِّئۡ لَنَا مِنۡ أَمۡرِنَا **رَشَدٗا** ١٠

Four properties: ____________________

Translation: ____________________

إِذۡ أَوَى ٱلۡفِتۡيَةُ إِلَى ٱلۡكَهۡفِ فَقَالُواْ رَبَّنَآ ءَاتِنَا مِن لَّدُنكَ رَحۡمَةٗ وَهَيِّئۡ لَنَا مِنۡ أَمۡرِنَا رَشَدٗا ١٠

Translation: ____________________

____